In memory of

Mary Catherine and Robert Emmet

JOHN LOCKE

W. M. SPELLMAN
Associate Professor of History
University of North Carolina at Asheville

First published 1997 by
MACMILLAN PRESS LTD
Houndmills, Basingstoke, Hampshire RG21 6XS
and London
Companies and representatives
throughout the world

ISBN 0–333–63421–7 hardcover
ISBN 0–333–63422–5 paperback

A catalogue record for this book is available
from the British Library.

This book is printed on paper suitable for recycling and
made from fully managed and sustained forest sources.

10   9   8   7   6   5   4   3   2   1
06   05   04   03   02   01   00   99   98   97

Printed in Hong Kong

Published in the United States of America 1997 by
ST. MARTIN'S PRESS, INC.,
Scholarly and Reference Division
175 Fifth Avenue, New York, N.Y. 10010

ISBN 0–312–16511–0 (cloth)
ISBN 0–312–16512–9 (paper)

1002282478

CONTENTS

PREFACE

The following brief study is presented as an introduction to some of the major issues which concerned John Locke from the Restoration until the beginning of the eighteenth century. In a synthetic work of this length no attempt is made at comprehension. I have relied very heavily on the valuable recent work of specialist scholars in the field of Locke studies throughout the book, and the bibliography provides some guidance for anyone wishing to explore particular questions in more detail and from a number of different perspectives. There has been an enormous expansion in the range and quantity of Locke scholarship over the last two decades as philosophers, political scientists, and historians continue to re-evaluate his many contributions to the intellectual life of the late seventeenth century and beyond. Hopefully something of the liveliness of the current debate over Locke's intentions will emerge from this survey; the reader should be cautioned that my own views are presented as one possible paradigm, but by no means the only one. The matter of Locke's religion and its relationship to his major published work has been the subject of increased scrutiny over the last decade, and I hope that what follows will affirm the general value of this new line of inquiry. Whenever appropriate, I have attempted to place Locke's work into an English and European historical context where religious conflict, or the memory of religious conflict, helped to shape most intellectual endeavours during the late seventeenth century. Beginning with a biographical overview in the first chapter, chapters 2 through 5 explore Locke's chief concerns in his work on epistemology, religion, education, and politics. The final chapter briefly charts the influence of Locke's work during the course of the eighteenth century, suggesting how the author's intentions were modified in a changing European and American historical context.

Two research fellowships, one funded by the William Andrews Clark Memorial Library at the University of California, Los Angeles, during the summer of 1995, and a second sponsored by the Obert and Grace A. Tanner Humanities Centre at the University of Utah during the

1995–6 academic year, allowed me to complete this project on schedule. A research leave and a faculty travel grant from my home institution, the University of North Carolina at Asheville, afforded me the opportunity to relocate and to write at two key periods. As with earlier projects my department chair, Bruce Greenawalt, unflinchingly supported my request for an off-campus research assignment. I wish to thank Carole Levin and Nancy Costello for reading and commenting on the text, my research colleagues at the Tanner Humanities Centre for listening and for criticizing, and Vivian Coman, Lynne Rasmussen and Greg Kemp for administrative support. Margaret Costello and Robert Burke, in their own inimitable styles, provided the requisite distractions at the right moments.

Salt Lake City
W.M.S.

ABBREVIATIONS FOR WORKS BY JOHN LOCKE

Correspondence   *The Correspondence of John Locke*, ed. E.S. De Beer, 8 vols (Oxford: Clarendon Press, 1976–89). Citations refer to volume and letter number.

ECHU   *An Essay Concerning Human Understanding*, ed. Peter Nidditch (Oxford: Clarendon Press, 1975). Citations refer to book, chapter, section.

ELN   *Essays on the Law of Nature*, ed. W. von Leyden (Oxford: Clarendon Press, 1954). Reissued 1988.

FT or ST   Respectively *First Treatise* or *Second Treatise* in *Two Treatises of Government*, ed. Peter Laslett (New York: Mentor Books, 1965). Citations refer to section numbers.

Paraphrase   *A Paraphrase and Notes on the Epistles of St. Paul to the Galatians, 1 and 2 Corinthians, Romans, Ephesians*, ed. Arthur W. Wainwright, 2 vols (Oxford: Clarendon Press, 1987). Citations refer to volume and page number.

STCE   *Some Thoughts Concerning Education*, ed. John Yolton and Jean Yolton (Oxford: Clarendon Press, 1989). Citations refer to section numbers.

Works   *The Works of John Locke in Ten Volumes* (London, T. Tegg, 1823).

INTRODUCTION

John Locke is perhaps best known today for his formulation and advocacy of a liberal political philosophy and for a theory of knowledge which emphasized the importance of environment in the learning process. Broadly speaking, he continues to be counted amongst those who inaugurated the eighteenth-century 'Age of Enlightenment' when, perhaps for the first time in the Western experience, the primacy and the dignity of the individual male were advanced in many spheres of human activity: religion, education, social organization, politics, and economic life. Locke's remarkable range of interests included not only political theory and epistemology, but carried over into the fields of medicine, economics, colonial administration, pedagogy, biblical commentary, and even botany. In an age when specialization was rare, Locke exhibited a remarkably varied professional competence reminiscent of the ideal of the Renaissance courtier. Something of the flavour of this diversity will be treated in the following survey, but the principal task at hand is to present a figure whose work, while revolutionary in terms of many of its proposals and subsequent influence, was in certain crucial respects very much of a piece with the traditional concerns of early modern Englishmen. And paramount among those concerns, eclipsing even his interest in the new science, was the intractable mystery of eternal life: the range of prospects beyond the grave, the sinner's role in securing the great reward, the nature of one's dependence upon both human and supernatural agency in translating what was an all-too-brief passage on earth into an unending and felicitous communion with the Creator.

This final issue, what might be spoken of as the problem of authority in religious and moral experience, engaged Locke's attention in each of his major published books. It was certainly the main concern of his greatest work, *An Essay Concerning Human Understanding* (1689), primarily because he was convinced that conflicting claims to authority in these two areas had in large measure perpetuated the social and political instability of his own day.[1] What constituted a legitimate basis for knowledge, belief, and conduct in an age when a wide variety

1

of claimants to authority presented themselves, often with force, before
the public? Not only were the myriad sources of purported authority –
Puritan conscience, Church of England tradition and ordained priesthood, sectarian 'inner light', absolutist 'divine right' theory, Catholic
infallibilism – conflicting in their attempts to clarify the nature of
man's proper relationship to God, but their dogged resistance to
allowing for any compromise had led, in Locke's view, to the very
serious disturbances of his youth, to the horror of civil war in a nation
where the righteous, guided by ideological absolutes, set themselves
against the equally righteous. Recently historians have begun to
acknowledge that the major crises of the seventeenth century in
England, 1637–42, 1678–83, and 1687–9, were not, as Whig historians
once held, about the triumph of parliaments, or as Marxist scholars
claimed, about the rise of capitalism and the bourgeoisie, but rather
about questions of religion and religious authority.[2] England before
1688 was very much a part of the on-going and supra-national
European struggle between Reformation and Counter-Reformation
ideals, and the origins of the great religious chasm could be traced, in
the end, to conflicting knowledge claims.

The seventeenth century in England was witness to a number of
significant upheavals, not the least of which involved a challenge to the
official Church as a central fixture of temporal and spiritual authority
and its replacement by a secular, and entirely this-worldly structure of
King in Parliament: that assembly of persons, parties, and institutions
which we now recognize as the early modern nation-state.[3] The
process of modern bureaucratic state building, as Theodore Rabb
and Richard Bonney have pointed out, was a Europe-wide phenom-
enon whose roots go back at least to the early sixteenth century.
Coincidentally, and tragically, the emergence of centralized states
which acknowledged no restraints on their autonomy occurred just
as European Christianity was fragmenting. The subsequent religious
conflicts reached their destructive nadir during Locke's youth, as the
Thirty Years War reduced the population of Central Europe by an
estimated 30 per cent.[4] Locke was deeply concerned about the
implications of expanding state power for the integrity of the individual's religious life, just as he was eager to preserve the initial
Protestant emphasis upon the responsibility of the individual, alone
before God in the most important business of life.

The chapter titles of this book suggest something of its main
organizing thread. I am certainly not the first to insist that Locke's
life must be viewed within the larger context of an interrelated theme

or project. While Locke, like most of his contemporaries, was an occasional writer in the sense that he was responding to particular problems as these arose in his own European and English culture, and while, like most of us, his views changed over the course of many years, certain distinctive themes and one overriding problem shaped his entire intellectual life.[5] I believe that this problem, the undertaking which united all of his diverse interests, was the clarification and solidification of a traditional Christian world-view during an age when the buttresses of the ancient faith were under severe strain from a number of quarters. A 2000-year-old cosmology, harnessed to the Christian story because of its comfortable comportment with a picture of creation emphasizing humankind's central station, had been decisively dismantled by the time of Locke's birth in 1632. Ancient geographical assumptions had been shattered by explorers who confirmed the existence of peoples around the globe who knew nothing of the 'universal' faith, and who in some cases seemed to behave in a manner which very much belied their lack of exposure to Christian norms. And the growth of commercial enterprise, joint stock companies and international trading mechanisms all called into question medieval assumptions regarding the applicability of one moral standard for all human activities. As an adult Locke would find himself involved in just the sort of economic activities which for centuries had been deemed inconsistent with Christian morality and the health of the individual soul. Religion and economics had by the seventeenth century become two separate kingdoms, each with antithetical rules governing conduct.[6] Locke's main concern, I am arguing, was with the former kingdom, but behaviour in the lesser one clearly informed one's prospects for the greater. Living appropriately in the terrestrial sphere, one's conformity with pre-established divine directions entailed sharp restrictions on the nature and extent of the freedom which is so often associated with Locke's name.

This approach to Locke, the emphasis upon a religious theme, may seem peculiar to those readers accustomed to viewing him through the prism of rationalism and secular politics, as indeed it would doubtless have seemed odd to many of those who claimed his mantle in the century following his death in 1704. Jean Le Rond d'Alembert, for example, in the introduction to the famous *Encyclopaedia*, credited Locke with founding 'scientific philosophy' just as his friend Isaac Newton was the father of 'scientific physics'. And Voltaire, certainly not one to celebrate apologists for traditional belief, considered Locke to be 'the Hercules of metaphysics', the man who shattered the complacency of the scholastic mind and the ossified pretensions of divine right theorists. In our own day Locke has been credited with overturning the notion, long at the centre of the Christian drama, that faith transcended the boundaries of frail human reason and provided the believer access to an empire of truth which was the soul's authentic home, what Aquinas so movingly called the 'vision of God'. In its place we have come to celebrate a man who, rising above the pressing concerns of his own immediate intellectual environment, magnified the power of human reason to an unprecedented level, banished mystery and emotion from the realm of mature discourse, and provided the foundation work for a new generation eager to discard the regressive encumbrance of a theological world-view.[7]

The argument of this book, that the Christian story and its vigorous, albeit innovative and at times controversial defence, constituted the core of Locke's main work, is predicated mainly on the philosopher's own extended efforts to discover the best means for passage into the next world, what constituted for all men and women of his generation the world of permanence and truth.[8] For Locke, as for all great Christian apologists over the centuries, 'the Condition of our Eternal Estate' was of pre-eminent concern, while the earthly experience was little more than a 'State of Mediocrity and Probationership', a pilgrimage where progress is measured in terms of one's personal discovery of and obedience to the dictate of divine law. As early as 1664 he had expressed the opinion that 'the world has nothing to give that is worthy of our prayers except the grave' and that before true happiness can be achieved 'nature must be done away with; these perishable and muddy coverings of the soul must be cast off'.[9] What follows is an effort to be guided by Locke's own words respecting what he took to be the fundamental concerns of his day, to avoid the interpretations of later commentators in an effort to appreciate the fact that the late seventeenth century, despite its usual association with the early Enlightenment, was still very much a society guided by an overwhelming religious impulse, a desire to know God, to forward His purposes, and to be with him at the close of one's earthly probation. As Nicholas Wolterstorff has recently reminded us, Locke's philosophy was informed by a deep Christian consciousness, and 'our common practice of treating seventeenth- and eighteenth-century European philosophers as if they were secular philosophers does most of them a very ill turn'.[10]

More than a set of actions and a type of engagement with one's fellows, seventeenth-century Christianity at its most basic level meant belief in an uncreated and ultimately benevolent Creator, in right and wrong originating in divine fiat, in reward and punishment outside the mundane tenure, in immortal life for all beyond the troublesome shadow of bodily death, and in the son Christ as saviour of a sinful humankind. Since the much loathed Muslims and much persecuted Jews both were committed to the first three concepts, it was the intervention of Christ into the human scene at the time of the Roman ascendancy, the overpowering significance of his salvific three-year mission in Palestine, which constituted the defining quality of the Christian experience. And in Locke's day, not only in England but across Western Europe, the divinity of the Christ, his co-eternal nature with the Father, not simply his wisdom or his unrivalled goodness, was thought to be emblematic of historic orthodoxy and key if his forgiving power were to be efficacious.

Christ's assumption of the human form, even 1600 years after the events detailed in the New Testament, continued to provide enormous emotional succour and satisfaction to pre-industrial people. Intellectual arguments for God, the intensive work of the very diligent scholastic fathers, had little appeal beside a humble story of personal intervention, a gratuitous visit of mercy undertaken in order to overturn the baleful consequences of the sin of the first Adam. To emphasize the personal connection in our relationship with the unmoved mover of the scholastic mind, to translate definitions of transcendence into the helping hand, the healing touch, the bond of simple flesh, the fear of rebuke and the longing for reward – this is what galvanized the on-going link between ordinary churchgoers and their God become man. And it was the character of Christ, his mercy, his willingness to turn the other cheek, but most importantly his acceptance of a painful propitiation on behalf of others, which, in the popular mind at least, eclipsed even the less-than-generous ascriptions of the sixteenth-century Calvinists and their Puritan offspring. Christ did discuss hell and provided for everlasting punishment in the Gospels, and while it would be unwise to discount the element of fear when treating motives to late seventeenth-century belief, it was the forgiving side of his nature – and the generous terms of forgiveness – that accounts for as much of his lasting appeal as did his threatening of endless fires.

Despite the fissure in the Western European Christian community brought about by the Reformation, lost hopes of a universal Christendom had the unintended result of intensifying discussion and debate over the essentials of belief and the requirements of religious practice preliminary to salvation. Piety and the meaning of orthodoxy, while never again matters of intellectual consensus after Luther's departure from his Augustinian order, nevertheless remained at the core of the Christian experience, with action or works viewed through the context of one's acceptance of truths beyond the purview of human reason. In a universe rather elaborately designed specifically as a stage for the on-going drama of salvation or damnation, where the First Cause had already set a date for the concluding event, and where the parameters of that event, while already known to God, were nonetheless shaped by individual faith and conduct, knowing the purport of God's intentions in His revealed word, 'getting it right' in the face of personal sinfulness, necessitated an almost extraordinary diligence and application. 'Issues long since encrusted over by centuries of philosophical commentary', one author has observed, were for the late seventeenth century 'matters of lively disputation among men convinced that the fate of their eternal souls rested upon a proper understanding of the world in which they lived.'[11] Scripture, after all, was made up of specific narratives, not general propositions and principles; God's intentions, His purpose for humankind, had to be drawn out of the stories by the reasonable and reflective mind.

Seventeenth-century thought has been described, rightly I think, as 'God-ridden'. Whenever a person wrote about 'the weather, the seasons, the structure of the earth, the constitution of the heavens, the nature of political society, the organization of the Church, social morality or ethics he was by definition taking up his pen to write about God'.[12] Locke's mature efforts to fashion a constitutional politics based on consent, his advice to friends on how best to educate their children into Christian morality, his reasoned pleas for complete toleration of Protestant dissent from the Established Church, his exploration of the limits of knowledge – were each designed not merely to forward the amelioration of existing material conditions in a society less than half a century away from the start of the industrial revolution, but more importantly to strengthen humankind's prospects for acceptance into the world of permanence and cohabitation with God. That his most significant work, *An Essay Concerning Human Understanding*, evidently began as a result of difficulties encountered by Locke and a small circle of friends over 'the principles of morality and revealed religion' suggests more than a little about where his pre-eminent intellectual interests remained throughout his adult life. The inward nature of things, knowledge of the divine will and the possibility of establishing a science of morality: these are the central themes of a work whose influence extends well beyond the confines of formal epistemology. For

anyone interested in the emergence of new forms of Christian apolo-
getic at a time when the impact of political, economic and scientific
change on English society was pronounced, a study of Locke's life and
principal ideas will not go unrewarded. Rejecting the traditional
language and methods of scholasticism, deeply impressed by the
empirical approach to science, an approach which had opened up a
new view of the physical universe distinct from the purposeful,
interventionist, and teleological one provided by medieval natural
philosophy, Locke would begin his investigation of human nature, and
human potential, on what actual behaviour showed it to be, not on
what traditional authority declared it to be. And building upon the
resulting investigation, Locke would reformulate the boundaries of
duty and action in an effort to reaffirm the ancient faith.

At the opening of the *Essay*, the understanding is described as 'the
most elevated Faculty of the Soul', and the soul was for Locke, as for so
many of his intellectual predecessors and contemporaries, the *imago dei*,
the spark of the divine within the human body. But while the understanding 'comes exceeding short of the vast extent of Things', while the
Essay sharply limits the purview of human knowledge, the highest
faculty of the soul is at least competent to secure our 'great Concern-
ments'. The business of mankind, he advised at the opening of the
work of which he was most proud, 'is not to know all things, but those
which concern our Conduct'.[13] And for Locke the question of conduct
– in social relations, in religious practice, in political behaviour, indeed
in each and every human activity – was the indispensable key, the
cornerstone to salvation. And Lockean notions of personal freedom
were always bound up with the standards set by God for human
action. Here was a perspective not entirely dissimilar from the voice of
traditional Anglican, and in particular latitudinarian, theology. It was
an outlook informed not in the least part by the disturbing fact of a
long-standing gulf between the professed belief and actual practice of
European Protestants. Arguments over what constituted the fundamentals of belief had, for over 1000 years, come to the same pass:
'schisms, separations, contentions, animosities, quarrels, blood and
butchery, and all that train of mischiefs which have so long harassed
and defamed Christianity'.[14] Locke's Christian England had, unfortunately, provided some of the worst examples of faith failing to work by
example, and for the man who was resigned to the fact that 'there are
very few lovers of Truth for Truths sake, even amongst those, who
persuade themselves that they are so', the job of reforming conduct
became the primary task of the enlightened Christian.[15]

In the end, the virtuous individual would be the most likely to respect the religious opinions and practices of his neighbour; he would be fitted to construct and to maintain a civil order and a national state whose roots were located in the free consent of the governed and whose main goal would be the protection of the individual and the improvement of the common welfare. Most importantly, the virtuous individual who learns the particulars of the law of nature and whose actions are consistent with them will secure for himself the greatest reward. Life was truly a probationary existence; meaning and transcendence were at the heart of the entire exercise. God remained the final superior and supreme legislator in a manner quite alien to modern Western culture where reasons for action have to do largely with social and economic utility. Whatever his disagreements with the customary methods of scholasticism, Locke's abiding faith in a purposeful universe directed by a God who punishes and rewards, where all things are created to serve a greater glory, where sinfulness and its opposite have unimaginable consequences, suggests that this spokesman for reason and enlightenment in the temporal sphere had rather larger motives for his life's work, larger certainly than it is often assumed by those who, for good or ill, claimed his inspiration in succeeding generations.

1

A LIFE OF COUNSEL

Locke was born in 1632, seven years after the accession of Charles I, and at the start of a decade when the King attempted to rule without the assistance of Parliament. He died in 1704, the loyal subject of Queen Anne and a man who had both witnessed and helped to shape the political and intellectual changes which transformed seventeenth-century England into a comparatively tolerant, politically powerful, and economically prosperous nation-state. He was born at Wrington in Somerset into an undistinguished family of local officials and landowners, some of whose predecessors had worked as clothiers and tanners. The village of Pensford, where he was raised, enjoyed a diversified economy where dairy farming, cattle grazing, brewing, and cloth making were undertaken in a labour-intensive setting. An emphasis upon the virtue of hard work, and a corresponding censure of idleness and vagrancy, was sounded from both the bench and the pulpit, with the minister who baptised Locke, Samuel Crook, expounding Scripture as the touchstone of God's intentions and as the basis of rules regulating conduct. Locke's father was a lawyer and small landowner whose fortunes never rose beyond the status of clerk to the justices of the peace in Somerset, but the Calvinist Presbyterian leanings of the elder Locke persuaded him that service in the parliamentary army during the Civil War was the only acceptable course for committed Protestants who saw the church of William Laud as the willing instrument of arbitrary royal authority. While unsuccessful in battle (Royalist forces quickly routed the parliamentary army in Somerset by June 1643) the philosopher's father was more fortunate in making the acquaintance – and securing the favour – of powerful friends. One of these, Colonel Alexander Popham, facilitated young Locke's acceptance at the prestigious Westminster School in 1647.[1]

Locke's move to London and his four years at Westminster under the tuition of its formidable master Richard Busby occurred at a moment in English history when the centuries-old tradition of monarchical rule had been shattered by the victory of Cromwell's army in the protracted Civil War. The execution of the King in 1649 and the subsequent 11-year republican experiment provided the political and religious backdrop against which Locke's public and university education took shape. Richard Busby's royalist and High Church sentiments, if not formative for the 15-year-old Locke, at least had the effect of challenging some of the Puritan tenets of his youth. Classical texts, not Reformation ones, were taught at Westminster. Locke would much later in life question the wisdom of public school education in general and the classical curriculum in particular, but his industry and success at Westminster led to his election to a Studentship at Christ Church, Oxford, in 1652, an unlikely rise for someone from Locke's modest background but also testimony to his exceptional intellectual skills. Once at university, Locke followed the traditional course of undergraduate study – Aristotelian logic, metaphysics, classical languages – pausing only to engage in informal contacts with friends like Richard Lower who were interested in natural philosophy and experimental medicine.[2] Locke was 20 at the time he was admitted to Christ Church, and as later reported by his friend Jean Le Clerc: 'He lost a great deal of time at the commencement of his studies because the only philosophy then known at Oxford was the peripatetic, perplexed with obscure terms and useless questions.'[3]

By the time he had completed the requirements for the BA degree in February 1656, Locke had grown weary of what he took to be the uncritical and authority-bound nature of traditional academic inquiry. Still his overall enthusiasm for the life of the mind led him to secure the MA in 1658, and after this date his commonplace books begin to provide a better picture of his developing interests. Locke's Studentship was tenable for life provided he did not marry and that he took holy orders once reaching a specific level of seniority in the College. Exceptions to these requirements were available for only four Studentships, known as Faculty Studentships, two being in law and two in medicine. Upon receiving the MA degree Locke was free to pursue his own intellectual interests, and it is now clear, thanks to the work of J.R. Milton, that the bulk of Locke's reading before leaving Oxford in 1667 was in the fields of medicine and chemistry.[4] His thoughts on questions of religion, ethics and politics may have become central to our appreciation of Locke as a philosopher in the centuries

since his death, but before the age of 35 he showed little sustained
interest in these matters, preferring instead the exciting possibilities
offered by the pragmatic control of nature.

The religious climate at Oxford during Locke's student years was
marked by the discipline of Puritan authorities who were eager to
reform what had been the headquarters of Charles I from 1642 until
1646. Royalist dons and heads of colleges were removed after the
triumph of the parliamentary cause, and a new pattern of attendance
at sermons and regular religious conversation with one's tutor was
mandated by those in charge. The Dean of Christ Church from 1656
to 1660 was John Owen, a formidable Calvinist and a member of the
assembly which had produced the Westminster Confession of Faith in
1646, but also a superior who refused to harry those who maintained
their sympathy for the old Anglican order as long as they kept their
opinions private. Locke's tutor was Thomas Cole, a man who later
became an important dissenting minister in London, but Cole's
influence over his student does not seem to have been significant.
Locke's 15 years of residence in the university city nurtured in him a
disdain for any type of enthusiasm in religion which discounted
rigorous intellectual foundations, and an equal suspicion of systems
of thought which equated mere tradition with veracity. His pursuit of
his medical interests (he eventually took an MB degree in 1674) was
motivated largely by his contacts with a growing circle of practitioners
who had rejected the Aristotelian and Galenic texts, men who were
concerned first and foremost with the empirical basis of illness. And
while his own medical interests were bookish and abstract before his
departure for London in 1667, the eagerness of physicians such as
Thomas Sydenham to observe how the body functioned was not
without its influence on Locke's subsequent desire to explore how
the mind acquired its ideas and knowledge.

We do not know exactly why Locke declined to take holy orders, but
his developing impatience with bodies of thought taught largely on the
basis of their ability to survive the test of time, coupled with his
participation in experimental science at the Oxford home of Robert
Boyle, doubtless contributed to his decision.[5] The inflexibility of
Puritan doctrine and practice during the years of his youth was
matched after 1660 by the intolerance and obduracy of the restored
Church of England. 'I have alwaies lookt on you as one of a higher
head then to take covert under a Cottage' was the advice of his
boyhood friend John Strachey respecting a career in the Church, 'and
in my opinion the best Country Parsonage is noe more.'[6] Even though

he was appointed lecturer in Greek at the University in 1660, Reader in Rhetoric at the end of 1662 and Censor of Moral Philosophy at the close of 1663, Locke's intellectual and spiritual interests were moving him beyond the confines of formal academic institutions where the parameters of acceptable discourse were sharply defined.

This is not to suggest that Locke's later defence of free thought, especially in the religious sphere, was firmly in place during those years when he held his Studentship at Christ Church. In fact, Locke's earliest writings on politics and religion (c.1660–2) indicate that he was very much in favour of the hard line taken by the re-established Church of England against all forms of dissent. If by toleration one meant the acceptance of 'enthusiasts' like the troublesome Quakers who disregarded social hierarchy and claimed for themselves special illumination and communication with God, if it meant allowing the self-indulgent and socially destructive behaviour of Ranters and Fifth Monarchy men who called for the end of all existing 'carnal' institutions, then Locke was fully prepared to welcome the interference of the state. The unpleasant experiential evidence of recent English history, and European history for that matter, indicated that differences over belief and practice had led straight to political discord and, ultimately, to military conflict. In the aftermath of Cromwell's death and the period of uncertainty which it promised, Locke's letters to family and friends reveal a man who was deeply troubled over his own – and the nation's – future prospects. 'O for a Pilot that would steare the tossed ship of this state to the haven of happinesse' he wrote to Thomas Westrow in the autumn of 1659.[7] His sole comfort at this time appeared to rest in his belief in divine providence and his trust in the prospect of eternal life once this chaotic passage was at a close. 'We are all Quakers here', he wrote in the aftermath of John Owen's abrupt dismissal as Dean of Christ Church, 'and there is not a man but thinks he alone hath this light within and all besides stumble in the darke.' God alone is 'the hand that governs all things, that manages our Chaos and will bring out of it what will be best for us'.[8]

Locke's discomfort over prospects for the future of the English polity were not unique. The hoped-for political recovery which the Restoration of the monarchy promised was mixed with a deep-seated and widespread anxiety over the task of reconstruction after 20 years of general instability. Restoration England, as Paul Seaward has written, was indeed 'a state on probation' as a mood of 'pessimistic conservatism' gripped those statesmen and citizens who yearned for a sense of permanence and security long absent from the political landscape.[9]

And the Church of England was an integral part of the effort to restore this stability, particularly in the minds of the members of the Cavalier Parliament. In a climate where it was widely believed that religious diversity had led to the political radicalism and contempt for authority witnessed during the previous two decades, the task of the official Church was to secure the support of people who had been free to choose from amongst a variety of sects during the Cromwellian period. The intense debates over precise theological issues which had marked the Interregnum were replaced after 1660 by clashes involving religious freedom and church–state relations. The question of how to treat dissent engaged a number of individuals in the months preceding and soon after the return of the King. Sometime in 1659 Locke had written to Henry Stubbe, also a former Westminster student and the author of a pamphlet in favour of a general toleration, expressing his scepticism over the willingness of people from different religious parties to unite peacefully under the same government.[10]

The following year, at the instigation of his Oxford friend Gabriel Towerson, Locke began to compose a rejoinder to Edward Bagshawe's *The Great Question Concerning Things Indifferent in Religious Worship* (1660), another pamphlet advocating the cause of toleration. On this occasion a strongly Royalist Locke insisted that the magistrate, even if he be one freely elected by the people, must be allowed to regulate the lives of his subjects even in areas where the word of God was silent, what contemporaries called 'indifferent things'. In a preface to his confutation of Bagshawe, Locke, in language which recalled the more trenchant fears of Thomas Hobbes, revealed that he had lived as if in a storm for most of his life and now looked forward to 'the approaches of a calm with the greatest joy and satisfaction'. If government were to guarantee this calm, however, it was essential that the minds of all subjects be habituated to obedience, not just in areas where the word of God was specific, but in all things deemed necessary by the magistrate. 'The subject is bound to a passive obedience', he insisted, 'under any decree of the magistrate whatsoever, whether just or unjust, nor, on any grounds whatsoever may a private citizen oppose the magistrate's decrees by force of arms.' Such a view, as Gordon Schochet has pointed out, 'did not question the pre-eminent importance of salvation' for Locke, but rather provided the conditions whereby everyone could pursue that objective in peace.[11] In the early 1660s, Locke's poor estimate of human nature was built firmly on the foundation of personal experience; the 'giddy folly' which had robbed Englishmen of stable government over the previous 20 years had to be disciplined. And the magistrate must be allowed to employ 'penalties and force' against anyone who would differ from the official Church. The brief but violent rising of religious radicals under Edward Venner in London in January 1661 seemed to confirm his scepticism and uneasiness.[12] And although he never published these early reflections on the need for unity in church and state (perhaps due to the fact that his vision of an intolerant church was fully realized by 1662), Locke's identification with Royalist authoritarianism, his equation of forbearance with licence, faction and rebellion, was unexceptional in its day. Obedience to authority had to be learned again, internalized, made part of one's affective and intellectual apparatus, if England were to reclaim its status as a cohesive and prosperous society, one where obedience to God's mandate for humankind could be pursued without disruption.

Locke's extracurricular interest in experimental medicine at Oxford, although it did not lead to a decision to enter the profession on a regular basis, contributed to what was perhaps the most significant career decision of his life. In the summer of 1666 Locke made the acquaintance of Anthony Ashley Cooper, first Baron Ashley, during the latter's visit to Oxford. The following year Lord Ashley invited the Christ Church don to serve as his personal physician in London, but after Locke's acceptance of the offer the relationship between the two men expanded to cover a wide range of religious and political affairs. Soon after his arrival Locke supervised a dangerous operation to remove a chronic hydatid abscess of the liver, and Shaftesbury credited him with saving his life. As personal secretary and adviser to one of the most powerful political figures of the Restoration period (Ashley was raised to the peerage as Earl of Shaftesbury in 1672 and served briefly as Lord High Chancellor), the Oxford man became engaged in a wide variety of activities on behalf of his patron and the circle of government opponents who worked after 1675 – sometimes in public but more often in secret – to curb the perceived absolutist and papist tendencies of Charles II. And it was during this period of intense political activity that Locke completed the political work for which he is best remembered today. Richard Ashcraft has argued convincingly in recent years that the older image of Locke as the detached college don, patiently defending religious toleration, contractual government, and an innovative theory of knowledge, is altogether mistaken. The philosopher's lasting contributions to epistemology, political theory, educational practice, and religious freedom arose not in isolation from the politics of Restoration England but as a product of one who was

immediately engaged in the major issues of the day.[13] Whatever his
other inconsistencies may have been, Shaftesbury was a strong opponent of arbitrary and absolutist government, and he always associated
Roman Catholicism with this form of temporal rule. Together with his
career-long call for toleration for Protestant Dissenters and in support
of the rights of Parliament, Locke's tenure as political confidant and
adviser in Shaftesbury's service was to prove a rich and productive
one.[14]

Restoration London was a city whose population was expanding
very rapidly. By 1700 about one tenth of the English people, or
575,000 individuals, resided in the capital city, a poor and youthful
population whose average life expectancy was 35 years and whose
means of survival differed sharply from the majority of the population
who continued to work the land. London was a commercial centre of
Europe at the time when Locke arrived from Oxford; overseas trade in
particular and business in general found much support among those
who had traditionally looked upon the land in terms of self-sufficiency
but who now saw the enormous possibilities of investment and profit-
making. Land management was improving and tenants and labourers
were called upon to think and to produce for a wider market. In the
city the poor, if they were fortunate, found employment in the building
trades, on the docks, in domestic work, in processing food and drink,
and in other service-sector undertakings. An agrarian and commercial
capitalist economy was in the process of displacing custom and
tradition as the fulcrum of the legal system, and while social order
and rank, deference and privilege were not being eroded in any
elemental sense, the basis of social status was shifting perceptibly as
wealth generated from sources other than the land played an increasing part in the economic life of the country.[15] Locke's appointments –
thanks to Shaftesbury's influence – as secretary to the Lords Proprietors of Carolina (1668–75) and secretary to the Council of Trade and
Plantations (1673–5) afforded him abundant first-hand exposure to
the changing political and economic face of England and the colonies.
From his perspective as an absentee landowner with an inherited
estate in Somerset generating a rental income of around £240 per
year, as an investor in the Royal African Company and the East India
Company, amongst other financial interests, Locke the gentleman also
had a sizeable personal stake in matters involving property and profit.
The industry and application to honest labour extolled in the Pensford
of Locke's youth, so essential to the improvement of the land and the
formation of a market economy, was readily embraced as an aspect of

the Fall as articulated in Genesis. But while Adam's descendants were forced to labour, God had also commanded them to subdue the earth and allowed them dominion over every living thing. The transformation of cities like London comported well with a Christianity which equated labour and enterprise with virtue and obedience.

Ashley was firmly opposed to the Clarendon Code, the set of repressive legislation against dissent passed by Anglican-dominated Parliaments in the first five years of the new reign. His position was largely a pragmatic one built upon economic considerations: persecution of peaceful Dissenters robbed the kingdom of some of the most enterprising and wealth-creating elements of the general population. For his part, Locke's first visit to the Continent in 1665 had afforded him an opportunity to witness the Calvinist, Lutheran and Catholic populations of Cleves living and working peacefully under one government, something he had thought unattainable only six years earlier in his letter to Henry Stubbe.[16] Soon after his arrival at Shaftesbury's home, Locke was encouraged to turn his attentions 'to the study of ecclesiastical and political affairs, which might have some relation to the business of a minister of state'.[17] Specifically, in an essay on toleration composed in late 1667 but never published during his lifetime, Locke expressed the revised position that speculative opinions and worship which did not affect politics or detract from the public good should *not* be regulated by the magistrate. Only atheism was singled out as an opinion not to be tolerated under any circumstances, and passive resistance to authority, although not active disobedience, was now allowed if the magistrate overstepped his power and imposed a conformity to one worship.

Locke's particular target in this essay was the Anglican policy of forcing one worship on Dissenters under pain of civil punishment; compulsion, he thought, betrayed little more than a conceit in one's own infallibility. He now seemed to acknowledge that outward forms of worship were an important part of an individual's communication with God.[18] Creating hypocrites by enjoining conformity to one set of opinions did nothing to strengthen national self-consciousness or the general prosperity of the state, and as long as one's personal religious beliefs and practice did not include the obligation to impose those beliefs or practice on others, then the civil government should permit a healthy diversity in religious thought and worship. Indeed the magistrate 'ought to do or meddle with nothing but barely in order to securing the civil peace and property of his subjects'.[19] Surely in the aftermath of the plague of 1665, the great London fire, and the disastrous naval war against the Dutch, this was the moment to reconsider the divisive official policy of intolerance. After the fall of the Earl of Clarendon in August 1667 a series of meetings took place in London between leading nonconformists and moderate churchmen who hoped to reach some agreement over comprehension, indicating that Locke was by no means alone in concluding the failure of persecution. In less than one decade, then, Locke had changed from a staunch defender of the Clarendon Code to one of its sharpest critics. In the process he had come to reject the Augustinian assumption that the true church could be recognized and unity of worship secured by frail mortals, that the first duty of the magistrate was to uphold religion or further anyone's spiritual well-being. Few of his Protestant contemporaries were prepared to accept the first position, while the Crown was not about to concede the second. It was an exceptional, indeed revolutionary, change of perspective, and one which would determine Locke's course on the matter for the rest of his life.

Locke's relocation to London and to Ashley's home on the Strand was also made easier by the fact that the hub of scientific activity based upon the experimental model was now located in the capital city. The new Royal Society served as a meeting place for researchers such as Robert Boyle and Dr Thomas Sydenham, and Locke was duly elected a Fellow of the Society in 1668. Boyle was the most articulate spokesperson for a growing conviction that scientific activity, particularly the task of demonstrating the power and wisdom of God in His handiwork, was a useful asset in the on-going battle against enthusiasm and irreligion, and Locke could draw comfort from the fact that the new science presented itself as a bulwark of traditional Christianity. The discipline and the caution advocated by the practitioners of the new science would later find their way into Locke's published works, where the emphasis upon the limits of human knowledge and the need for humility and faith in light of human ignorance would become one of the core elements of the philosopher's message.[20] What can we know, how do we regulate our assent when we lack knowledge, and for what ends should we engage our fragile powers? These questions would later emerge as central issues for Locke, and his contacts with the men of affairs and the men of science in London after 1667 doubtless helped him to clarify their significance for his own turbulent age.

Another positive, albeit unanticipated, result of Locke's transfer from Oxford to London was the establishment of contacts with a group of Anglican divines who were reluctant to pursue the exclusionary and persecutory strategy of the re-established Church. Locke's reading at

Oxford on religious subjects had covered three basic areas: biblical scholarship, patristics, and Anglican theology. There is no evidence in the commonplace books to suggest that he disagreed with the theological perspective of Anglican authors such as Henry Hammond, John Pearson, and Richard Hooker, but unfortunately we do not know about his church-going at this or at any other time in his life.[21] What is clear is that by 1668 he had come to know the Platonist and former Vice-Chancellor of Cambridge University, Benjamin Whichcote. Appointed vicar of St Lawrence Jewry in that year, Whichcote's simple style and focus on the essentials of Scripture as understood by reason was endorsed by a company of younger Cambridge graduates who had taken up livings in the city after the Restoration. John Tillotson, Simon Patrick, and Edward Fowler were three of the more notable figures who would later achieve prominence at the episcopal level after the Glorious Revolution, but in the 1660s their critics attached the derisive label 'latitudinarian' to their theology and their politics. Interested primarily in the prospect of 'comprehending' moderate Dissenters into a broadly based Church of England, the latitudinarians argued that such a comprehension indeed was possible if the simple essentials of the faith, and not the particular ceremony and doctrine of the official Church, were made the criteria by which one enjoyed membership in a national communion.[22] Amongst the requirements that the latitudinarians were willing to forgo in order to enlarge the Church, perhaps the most significant was the call for ministers previously ordained by Presbyterians to undergo reordination at the hands of a bishop. A scheme for a comprehension, mentioned earlier, was actually drawn up in 1667 and another was introduced in Parliament in 1674, but despite the support of some MPs and government ministers, the majority in Parliament refused to make substantive concessions to the nonconformist community, most MPs continuing to equate religious dissent with political treachery. As one member put the matter in 1669, anyone proposing changes in the religious settlement should 'come as a proposer of new laws did in Athens, with ropes about their necks'.[23] At no time before the Glorious Revolution did the prospect of even the mildest compromise with dissent engage the support of the political nation, much less the approval of Archbishop of Canterbury Sheldon (1663–77) or his successor William Sancroft (1677–91), and the Crown's clumsy efforts to force the issue with declarations of indulgence for Catholics and Dissenters in 1662 and again in 1672 only hardened parliamentary resistance to change.

Locke became friends with a number of latitudinarian divines after 1667, including Tillotson, Fowler, Isaac Barrow, and Gilbert Burnet. His final library included over 100 separate works by latitudinarians, while his journal entries, commonplace books and unpublished theological manuscripts all indicate a familiarity with the work of these authors.[24] In large measure the latitudinarians defended their willingness to relax the requirements for entry into the official communion on the basis of a moderate scepticism growing out of the late sixteenth-century rule of faith controversy. The latitudinarian emphasis on the importance of behaviour as a key component of belief (a working faith) and their insistence that Revelation was very much a restatement of natural law, also proved attractive to Locke. Still, despite the emergence of these new friendships, Locke did not devote much time to theological inquiry before the age of 50. The bulk of his writing in this area would await his exile to Holland in 1683, and it would expand considerably during the final 15 years of his life.

Locke's position on the proper relationship between church and state had, then, altered dramatically in just a few short years after the Restoration settlement. Whether or not this fundamental shift would have occurred had he remained in residence at Christ Church is, of course, impossible to know. It is clear, however, that his exposure to Ashley's advocacy of toleration on economic grounds, his brief diplomatic foray to Brandenburg where he viewed political union in the midst of religious diversity, and his developing friendship with the major experimental scientists and latitudinarian divines in London, worked to modify his views in a direction where few of his countrymen were prepared to tread, ultimately even beyond the latitudinarian ideal of a inclusive yet obligatory national Church. Once the restoration of the monarchy had been secured, the remnants of the Interregnum army disbanded, and the government's staying power successfully tested (during the second Dutch war), once the historic interplay between Parliament and Crown had been restarted after a decade of executive authoritarianism and the free reign of sectarian enthusiasm, Locke began to reassess his earlier views on what he always took to be the most important business in life: the means for securing everlasting life in a realm where humankind was no longer finite.

In fact the great *Essay Concerning Human Understanding* owes its origins in part to this crucial period of reappraisal. When Samuel Parker's *A Discourse of Ecclesiastical Polity* appeared in print in 1670, forcefully asserting the need for the imposition of religious orthodoxy, Locke decided to undertake an examination of the epistemic foundations of the case for imposition. Professor Ashcraft has argued that questions of epistemology were for Locke directly related to the potential sweep of legitimate state power. How, Locke would ask, could one know with certainty what was required in religious belief and observance, and if this knowledge was not within reach, then what limits did this impose upon the civil authorities? At a time when Parliament was redoubling its efforts to stamp out nonconformity by passing a more rigorous Conventicle Act, Locke began to look at the very roots of knowledge claims, and he would continue the endeavour over the next 20 years.[25] We will look at the results of his inquiries in the next chapter.

After nine years in residence at Ashley's home, Locke undertook his first extensive trip to the Continent, choosing France as his place of residence. He remained in Louis XIV's kingdom for the next three years, travelling, making new friends and meeting with distinguished scholars and physicians.[26] His notes during this period indicate both an awareness of the growing restrictions being placed upon French Protestants by the government, and a revulsion against the all-embracing absolutism of Louis XIV. When he returned to England in the spring of 1679 his patron (now Lord Shaftesbury) was at the head of a parliamentary campaign to exclude the Catholic James, Duke of York, from succeeding to his brother's throne. Locke's experiences in Catholic and absolutist France were fresh memories indeed when he resumed his service under Shaftesbury. Throughout the 1670s, and especially after James's conversion to Roman Catholicism became public knowledge in 1673, fears of Catholic conspiracy and its absolutist political character began to dominate political discourse, with rumours of ministerial corruption and complicity with Catholic recusants exacerbating tensions. With the panic atmosphere created by the Popish Plot in 1678, elections for Parliament in February 1679 returned members committed to rooting out corruption at Court and resolved to deny James his right to succeed to the throne. Shaftesbury had been recruited into the government as lord president of the council by Charles in an effort to defuse the situation, but parliamentary intransigence led to a stalemate, the rapid dismissal of Shaftesbury from the council, and the prorogation of the second 'Exclusion' Parliament in October 1679.[27]

Throughout the course of the next two years as the campaign to investigate the Popish Plot and to exclude James moved from the parliamentary stage to the popular press and then into the streets of London, Locke worked closely with Shaftesbury and completed a draft of what would be published in 1689 as *Two Treatises of Government*.[28] His friend James Tyrrell published his *Patriarcha Non Monarchia* (1681), a book devoted to rebutting Sir Robert Filmer's extreme royalism, at the time that Locke was thinking about the subject of *Two Treatises*.[29] Loyalist opponents of exclusion – including bishops who had no enthusiasm for the prospect of a Catholic monarch whose perceived sympathy for arbitrary government threatened English habits of governance – defended the Duke of York out of a strong sense of commitment to the principle of monarchical legitimacy. The government attempted to portray champions of exclusion as radical Dissenters bent upon repeating the disasters of the Interregnum, men who would destroy royal power and the balanced constitution, incendiaries who had no respect for law and tradition. The radical nature of Locke's *Two Treatises* can perhaps best be appreciated when set against the fact that exclusionists, for the most part, sought only to make one emergency alteration to the order of succession in the interests of preserving the Protestant nation. There was no wish on the part of moderate exclusionists to forward a contract theory of government whereby the right to revolution was placed squarely in the hands of the political nation.[30] Locke's patron may have been one of the more prominent leaders of exclusion, but he was by no means a representative opponent of James's right to succeed his brother. By the spring of 1681, after another clash between exclusionists and the Crown at a one-week parliamentary session held in Oxford, the government engineered an effective propaganda campaign against the parliamentary opponents of James, and in November 1682 a sickly Shaftesbury, after Tory candidates took control of the office of Lord Mayor and the two sheriffs' posts, fled the country for exile in the Netherlands, where he died the following year. Locke had been in residence at Christ Church during that final 'Exclusion' Parliament, securing accommodation for Shaftesbury and his entourage and observing the intransigence of the King on the issue of the succession. The failure of the Whigs at this juncture was critical to Locke's future.

Charles II's resolve proved the undoing of his erstwhile minister and placed Shaftesbury's former adviser in the worst of possible situations. After two years in which the Whig cause was subverted by a systematic campaign to confiscate and reissue town charters, and by what one scholar has called a 'vicious Tory putsch' in London, Locke decided to quietly withdraw from England.[31] The failure of the Rye House Plot and the subsequent trial and execution of Algernon Sydney both for his complicity in the attempt to kidnap Charles and James and as the

author of seditious manuscripts (a rebuttal of Sir Robert Filmer's
Patriarcha published posthumously as *Discourses on Government*) would
have understandably alarmed Shaftesbury's former secretary and
author of a radical, even seditious, anti-absolutist manuscript. Equally
disturbing for Locke would have been the July 1681 execution of
Stephen College, another Shaftesbury supporter convicted of distri-
buting anti-monarchical literature in Oxford.

The next six years in Holland provided Locke with an opportunity
for prolonged reflection and writing on the major philosophical and
religious issues which would engage him for the remainder of his life.
He developed a number of close friendships with liberal Dutch
thinkers, the most important being Philipp van Limborch, professor
of divinity at the Remonstrants' seminary in Amsterdam, Jean Le
Clerc, also on the faculty of the same institution, and Benjamin Furly,
an English-born Quaker who had established himself as a successful
businessman in Rotterdam. Limborch later recalled that when Locke
had heard that he was a professor of theology among the Remonstrants
'he introduced himself to me, and we afterwards had many conversa-
tions about religion, in which he acknowledged that he had long
attributed to the Remonstrants doctrines very different from those
which they held, and now that he understood what they really were,
he was surprised to find how closely they agreed with many of his own
opinions'.[32] Each of these men rekindled Locke's interest in religious
study after the years of political engagement in Shaftesbury's service.
It was during this period that Locke began purchasing and reading
works of Socinian (or Unitarian) theology. His friend Damaris Cudworth was both pleased and surprised by the depth of his reading in
theology while in exile, playfully rebuking him for sending her letters
'not to be understood without turning to St Paul, and St Peters
Epistles'.[33] Locke kept company mainly with theologians and clerics
during his years in Holland, perhaps expecting never to return to
England and undoubtedly moved to consider larger issues than the
whirl and tumble of national politics on an island at the periphery of
Western Europe.

The Dutch Remonstrants were the intellectual heirs of a group of
religious rationalists or Arminians who had presented a request to the
States General in the year 1610 calling for greater toleration in
religious affairs. Condemned by the Synod of Dort in 1619, they
continued to meet although they never attracted a popular following.[34] Both Limborch and Le Clerc were advocates of a minimalist
theology where behaviour counted for more than a particular belief in

the great quest for salvation, and their company reanimated Locke's exploration of the merits of toleration in a pluralist society where the task of government was to forward the common civil interests of the community. That spirit of toleration was not to be found back at Christ Church, where Locke was stripped of his Studentship by royal command in November 1684. By the following February Charles II was dead, and Shaftesbury's old nemesis the Duke of York succeeded peacefully to the throne, an anxious nation hoping that the new monarch's personal beliefs would not intrude themselves into affairs of state. In this, of course, all were mistaken, as James quickly proceeded to alienate what began as perhaps the most loyal Parliament since the Restoration.[35] In the wake of the failed Monmouth invasion of July 1685, the government intensified its efforts to hunt down conspirators living in Europe. Locke's name appeared on a list presented to the States General for arrest and return for prosecution, while in the south of England Judge George Jeffreys condemned 400 peasant rebels to death and deported 1200 more to Barbados. By November James had prorogued Parliament and inaugurated his disastrous three-year project to Catholicise the realm, all in the shadow of Louis XIV's revocation of the Edict of Nantes (October 1685) which resulted in the flight of many persecuted Huguenots to Britain and the Netherlands.

Although the English authorities under James made some attempt to extradite him in 1685, and while he was obliged at one point to go underground and adopt an assumed name (Dr van der Linden), Locke's years of forced exile in Holland were highly productive ones. At the very moment when political matters which would have been of deep concern to the author of the *Two Treatises* claimed the attention of his countrymen, Locke was able to focus his intellectual energies on religious and philosophical issues. During the months between the loss of his Studentship and the death of Charles II, he was busy in Utrecht working on the manuscript of his *Essay Concerning Human Understanding*. In addition, a series of extensive letters written to his friend Edward Clarke between 1684 and 1688 on the subject of educating Clarke's children later became the basis for *Some Thoughts Concerning Education* (1693). Locke also served as a regular contributor and reviewer of theological books for Le Clerc's new journal of ideas, *La Bibliothèque Universelle*, and in late 1685, less than a year before James II issued his first Declaration of Indulgence permitting Catholics and nonconformists freedom of worship, Locke set to work on a brief Latin essay on religious toleration. This *Epistola de Tolerantia*, dedicated to Limborch,

was written with a European audience in mind at the very moment
when a Catholic monarch had assumed the throne in England and
while his counterpart in France was pursuing a brutal policy of
repression against Protestant inhabitants. Fearful that a resurgent
Catholicism was now in a strong position to overturn by force the
work of Protestant reform across Western Europe, Locke argued that
coercion was never a legitimate mechanism for saving souls and that
government's exclusive charge was to secure the lives and the property
of the people.[36] James's Declaration, while apparently concurring with
this argument, was in fact merely a calculated effort to win the support
of non-Anglicans in the King's struggle to obtain an amenable
Parliament. Few Dissenters were willing to affix their hopes on the
promises of a Catholic monarch whose unilateral decrees, if successful
at this juncture, might be easily reversed by the same opportunistic
voice at a later date. In *A Letter to a Dissenter*, published in the summer
of 1687, George Savile, Marquis of Halifax, reminded Protestant
nonconformists that their freedom, if purchased at the price of destroy-
ing the established law, would provide scant long-term security, and
he urged Dissenters to make common cause with the Church of
England in return for a future comprehension or toleration.[37]

Between 1687 and 1689, as events in England reached a crisis point,
Locke lived quietly in Rotterdam as a household guest of the Quaker
Benjamin Furly. Born in Colchester in 1636, Furly had become a
follower of George Fox in 1650, and his behaviour after his conversion
fits perfectly the very negative picture of Quakers that Locke held
during those years. Although Furly's temper had mellowed with age, it
is perhaps one measure of how far Locke's views on religious toleration
had evolved since 1660 that he could take up lodging and become close
friends with a man whose extreme position on human equality in the
mid 1650s had infuriated even Fox.[38] Locke's manuscript proposal for
a 'Society of Pacifick Christians', composed in 1688, would have been
pleasing to a man of Furly's background and guiding principles. The
document spoke favourably of 'the light which enlightens every man'
and the requirement that religion in such a society enjoin only 'the
duties of a good life'. The document presented a model for the dignity
of the individual conscience which was very much at odds with recent
state policies in both France and England.

James's efforts to advance Catholicism by royal decree faced increasing opposition, particularly after he requested further monies
from Parliament in order to keep his 20,000-man army in place after
the defeat of the Monmouth rebels. As military commissions were

transferred to Catholics, heads of colleges at the two universities dismissed and replaced by Catholic supporters of the King, local borough charters threatened with revocation, shire officials supplanted, and, in May 1688, leading prelates of the Church of England prosecuted for seditious libel, the pattern of arbitrary behaviour which had always been alleged against James now seemed obvious to Whigs and Tories alike. And while the King and Queen Mary celebrated the birth of a male heir in June, hopes evaporated that Catholic extremism would end once the crown passed peacefully to James's Protestant daughter Mary and her husband William of Orange. Locke's endorsement of the right to revolution, originally composed in the midst of a drive to exclude James, would have seemed something other than extreme had it been in print for the edification of those Whig politicians who now urged William to rescue and preserve the Protestant faith in England.

But it was not in print. In fact, when he finally returned to England in January of 1689, in the company of the Queen's entourage and safely after the ignominious departure of James II, Locke was, in terms of his intellectual standing, little more than a 56-year-old exile scholar who had published nothing of consequence. The extraordinary appearance at the close of that year of his three most significant works, *An Essay Concerning Human Understanding*, *Two Treatises of Government*, and *A Letter Concerning Toleration*, inaugurated what can be viewed as the final stage of Locke's career, a 15-year period in which he balanced a number of important public duties with further publishing efforts and lengthy defences of his main epistemological and religious ideas. William's assumption of executive power after the flight of James II, and the controversial decision of the Convention Parliament to declare the throne vacant, signalled the beginning of a new era in England as the King quickly brought English military power to bear in the wider Continental struggle against Louis XIV. Locke was offered a diplomatic post in the new government, but he declined the invitation and accepted instead a modest appointment as a Commissioner of Appeals. He lived in London for the next two years, observing with some disappointment the failure of Parliament to act on the proposed 'comprehension' and 'toleration' bill for nonconformists, even though the final Toleration Act granted relief from persecution to Dissenters while denying them full civil equality.[39] Those years seemed to have been filled with political activity, advising friends such as the Earl of Pembroke, Lord Monmouth, Solicitor-General John Somers, and MPs Edward Clarke and Sir William Younge, among others. 'I find myself so occupied with public affairs and the concerns of my friends that I am hardly able to touch a book now', he wrote to Limborch as early as April 1689, hoping 'I shall be able one day to return to my old and agreeable ease in the world of letters.'[40]

That opportunity came closer to realization during 1691 when he relocated his principal place of residence to Essex and the home of Francis and Damaris Masham. Locke had known Damaris Masham since 1682, when he was 50 and she just 24. She was the daughter of the distinguished Cambridge Platonist Ralph Cudworth, and their early letters bespeak a strong romantic attachment. Damaris was also an intellectual who, despite her appreciation of Locke's strong empiricism, never entirely abandoned her interest in the mystical aspects of Cambridge Platonism. In 1685 she had married Sir Francis Masham, a widower with eight children, but her friendship with Locke remained undiminished during the remainder of the philosopher's exile. After a number of extended visits to the Masham's Tudor manor house in Oates near High Lavar (near Harlow), Locke accepted an invitation to move into two rooms on the first floor as a paying guest. Here, during the final 12 years of his life, he continued to write and correspond widely, journeying the 20 miles to London whenever business (he was appointed to the newly formed Board of Trade in 1696) required his presence.

There were many visitors to Oates during these final years. The most illustrious was Isaac Newton, whom Locke had met at the Earl of Pembroke's London home in 1689. Their strongest mutual interest turned out to be theology, especially biblical interpretation, and both men dedicated themselves to the task. Newton was one of a small group of readers who encouraged Locke to publish his extensive manuscript on St Paul's Epistles. The major fruits of Locke's inquiries into New Testament study involved these extensive notes and paraphrases on the Epistles of St Paul, but although he finally prepared the text for the press the *Paraphrase and Notes on the Epistles of St. Paul* did not appear in print until after his death.[41] Newton also assisted Locke in the summer of 1692 by reviewing the manuscript of Locke's *Third Letter for Toleration*, a 300-page response to Jonas Proust's critique of the original 1689 *Letter*.[42] After the near simultaneous publication of what were to become his most influential works in 1689, Locke set himself to composing a work on economics, published in 1693 as *Some Consideration of the Consequences of the Lowering of Interest, and Raising the Value of Money*. During 1693 he was also engaged in the preparation of a new edition of the *Essay*, a work which was being read at Trinity

College, Dublin, and for which, at Jesus College, Oxford, John Wynne asked Locke's permission to design an abridgment for student use. In that same year *Some Thoughts Concerning Education* made its way into the bookshops, and in 1695 his enormously controversial *The Reasonableness of Christianity* reached the public. Locke never acknowledged his authorship of this last work, nor did his name appear on the title page of *Two Treatises* or *A Letter Concerning Toleration*. Apparently the controversy which soon surrounded his *Essay*, a work Locke did acknowledge as his own, provided more than ample explanation for his refusal to affirm what was common knowledge by the end of the century. The fact that the Licensing Act, which had lapsed in 1695, did nothing to protect radicals like Thomas Aikenhead, the Edinburgh student who was hanged for ridiculing the Scriptures, and the fact that the Blasphemy Act of 1697 aimed to exclude religious radicals from public office, certainly were not lost on Locke.[43] On more than one occasion he sharply rebuked even his closest friends when they appeared to betray the poorly kept secret regarding his authorship. The contractarian argument contained in the *Two Treatises*, together with the call for ending the church–state alliance contained in the *Letter*, placed Locke, whether he approved of the association or not, squarely in the camp of those intent upon reducing the power of the state by attacking the monopoly privileges of the Church of England. As J.C.D. Clark has argued, 'the ubiquitous agency of the State was the Church' even after the passage of the Toleration Act. Since the Church enjoyed control over education and access to political office, any argument which denied the exclusive right of the official communion to define religious orthodoxy ultimately struck at the power of the State which supported that communion.[44]

Almost as soon as Locke's work began to appear in print it was the subject of close and extended scrutiny. Before the publication of the *Essay* in December 1688, for example, an abridgment which had appeared in the January issue of Jean Le Clerc's *Bibliothèque Universelle* had drawn harsh censure from churchmen who thought that Locke's epistemology undermined traditional Christian sources of knowledge. Locke did not take this criticism very well, despite his comments in the preface to *Some Thoughts Concerning Education* and in the 'Epistle to the Reader' of the *Essay* where he admits that his work contains mistakes and calls for his readers to suggest improvements. Normally Locke's friends were supportive, and this support was much appreciated by the author. But whenever strangers raised doubts, Locke either refused to respond or did so in a terse and quarrelsome manner.

There were some exceptions to his routine rejection of criticism. When *The Reasonableness of Christianity* appeared in print in 1695, the clergyman John Edwards accused the author of Socinianism, a heresy imported from the Continent which stressed the unity of the godhead and the complete rationality of the Christian faith. Edwards, a former Cambridge Fellow, was an intemperate and tendentious adversary, but the fact that Locke felt obliged to answer the charge against him is an indication of how anxious he felt about maintaining his credentials as an orthodox layman, particularly in light of his friendship with known anti-trinitarians such as Thomas Firmin and William Popple. He wrote two *Vindications* of his book on religion, each of which denied the charge of Socinianism but in a tone duplicating Edwards's unseemly polemical style. When the Grand Jury of Middlesex banned *The Reasonableness* in 1697, it was one indication of how little success these rejoinders had in assuaging public opinion.

Unfortunately, no sooner had Locke engaged the irascible Edwards in debate than a much more formidable opponent, Edward Stilling-fleet, Bishop of Worcester, took up the cause of identifying the unorthodox implications of the work that Locke was most proud of: *An Essay Concerning Human Understanding*. Stillingfleet wisely refrained from charging Locke with Socianianism, a word closely associated with atheism in the late seventeenth century, but in his *Discourse in Vindication of the Doctrine of the Trinity* (1696), the bishop warned that the epistemology of the *Essay* contributed to the strength of the anti-Trinitarian movement. Stillingfleet later alleged that Locke's new 'way of ideas' left no room for the traditional Christian definition of the nature of knowledge and, in particular, knowledge of immaterial substances like the soul. Locke and James Tyrrell had tangled with Stillingfleet before over the question of toleration during the Exclusion crisis, but when it came to the orthodoxy of the *Essay*, the bishop was too important a figure to ignore. Locke's three replies to Stillingfleet's letters, written between 1697 and 1698, are lengthy defences of his Christian credentials, defences written near the close of a decade when advocates for a non-Scriptural religion pressed their case with unparalleled vigour. We will survey Locke's exchange with the Bishop of Worcester in more detail in chapter 3 since the points in dispute between them highlight the parameters of Locke's mature theology.

The most prominent of the late seventeenth-century advocates of a faith without mystery were the Deists. The controversy surrounding their ideas claimed the attention of numerous churchmen worried lest the appeal to reason which was the hallmark of that special perspective should obviate the need for faith in a miracle-working and providential God. Just as the authority of arbitrary magistrates was called into question in 1688, just as the Toleration Act of 1689 officially ended the Church of England's monopoly over the religious affairs of the nation, allowing Trinitarian Protestants freedom to follow their conscience outside the disciplinary power of the national Church, the Deists intensified their challenge to the traditional authority of Scripture as the sole touchstone of the divine mandate, replacing that Reformation era guidepost with all-sufficient reason. Revelation was held up to be an inadequate and hopelessly controversial instrument of moral and spiritual enlightenment by the Deists, and the religion of reason was proposed as an appropriate corollary to a civil order based upon consent. Where Newton's physics promised simplicity and harmony at the cosmic level, Deism offered the same benefits within the realm of the spirit, leaving mankind with a God who was simply a prime mover, uninterested in meddling with His creation, and one who would never entrust his message to the ignorant fishermen featured in the New Testament. In an age when polemical tracts and pamphlets were commonplace, when an informal and direct style appealed to the ordinary reader, the Deists were quick to take advantage of the press as a means of advancing their controversial message of a Christianity purified from the superstitious accretions of the ages. Charles Blount had led off the assault in the 1680s, but the full impact of the movement was only felt in the following decade, when even the mildest dissent from orthodoxy was associated with deistical freethinking.

As long as the latitudinarian divines were keen to declare the rational nature of their faith and the competence of reason to evaluate Revelation, as long as Archbishop of Canterbury John Tillotson could claim that the appeal to reason posed no threat to the Church of England, and as long as there was no single cohesive group of Deists who adhered to a uniform programme, it was not a difficult task for nervous churchmen to associate Locke's views with an emergent heterodoxy such as Deism. His pleas for toleration, his disdain of enthusiasm, his reduction of the essentials of the faith in *The Reasonableness of Christianity*, his dissent from orthodoxy regarding the origin of ideas and the nature of human knowledge in the *Essay*, and his association with anti-trinitarians, all contributed to the intensity of the debate surrounding his work. What had begun as the employment of reason in religion in pursuit of an erenical Church ended with the Deist assault upon an allegedly covetous and irrational priestly class.

When the young Irishman John Toland published his *Christianity Not Mysterious* (1696) with the express purpose of abolishing the need for Revelation, his employment of Locke's definition of knowledge and the overall epistemology of the *Essay* unfortunately linked the philosopher with one of the more vocal protagonists in the Deist controversy.[45]

'I hope to make it appear that the use of reason is not so dangerous in religion as it is commonly represented', Toland had announced in the preface to his book, and on this point he was in common cause with Locke and his latitudinarian friends. In fact Toland was keen to link his ideas not only to Locke but to the latitudinarian bishops. The title page to *Christianity Not Mysterious* includes a quote from Tillotson, who had died in 1693 and whose passing Locke lamented as leaving him 'scarcely anyone whom I can freely consult about theological uncertainties'.[46] Deism appropriated much of the latitudinarian message, forcing men like Locke to struggle to clarify their appropriation of reason for the defence of traditional Christianity. In publishing his *Reasonableness of Christianity*, Locke had laboured with 'some hope of doing service to decaying piety, and mistaken and slandered Christianity'. But having to defend the work against the aspersions of men like Edwards, in addition to clarifying his purpose in the *Essay* for the benefit of the Bishop of Worcester, was, for Locke, an enormously frustrating and unilluminating employment.

In 1700, at the age of 72, increasingly troubled by asthma and bronchitis and having been absent from many meetings of the Board of Trade, Locke withdrew from all political affairs. Limborch commended his friend's decision to spend his declining years 'in rest, study and religious meditations'.[47] From 1696 until 1700 his duties on the Board had necessitated living in London over long periods, mostly in the late summer and early autumn, and these trips to the City had often exhausted him. From Oates he continued to monitor domestic and international developments, particularly the efforts of King William to build a new anti-French coalition. Friends and acquaintances visited the old man at the Masham household on a regular basis, and when he was not entertaining Locke would devote a good portion of his private moments to answering critics and to religious exercises, especially work on his paraphrases and notes on St Paul's epistles. Writing to his Irish friend William Molyneux in April 1698, Locke doubted whether he should trouble the press with new matter, 'or, if I did, I look on my life as so near worn out that it would be folly to hope to finish anything of moment in the small remainder of it'.[48] He continued to take an active interest in the children of his closest friends, and on more than one occasion the son and daughter of Edward Clarke, for whom Locke had written *Some Thoughts Concerning Education*, enjoyed extended stays at Oates. Locke also began to show a special concern for the career of his cousin Peter King, a young man in his twenties, advising him on everything from politics (King was elected MP for Bere Alston in 1701) to financial investments and matrimony. King would eventually become Lord High Chancellor of England, and Locke treated him in a fatherly fashion, making King his heir and, in his will, entrusting him with one half of his final library of books and all of his personal manuscripts.

In the year before his death, as the war against Louis XIV's absolutist and expansionist pretensions resumed in Europe, three events occurred which in a sense highlighted something of the significance of Locke's lifelong contribution to the enlargement of human freedoms: personal, intellectual and political freedoms. In 1703 Tory politicians tried but failed to push through a bill designed to suppress 'occasional conformity', the practice whereby Dissenters in public offices, by taking communion in the Church of England at least once each year, had avoided the exclusionary provisions of the Test Act. In the wake of Parliament's failure to grant full civil equality to Protestant Dissenters with the 1689 Toleration Act, Locke was not alone among Whigs in his sympathy for this rather transparent abuse of church membership. A second bill, again proposed by Tory MPs, sought to restrict the liberty of the press, in particular the Whig press. This too failed to win passage, although the fragility of the victory won with the end of the Licensing Act in 1695 could not have been lost on men like Locke. Finally, in the same year when domestic politics took a turn for the affirmation of authority over liberty, in Oxford a move was proposed by heads of colleges to prohibit tutors and students from reading Locke's *Essay*. Surprisingly, the occasion for the proposal was not allegations of heterodoxy in the text, but instead a worry that Locke's strictures against traditional logic and university disputations were eroding confidence in true and time-tested methods of instruction. The proposal ultimately came to nothing, but not before Locke had written wryly to his young friend Anthony Collins that rationality 'is so glorious a thing that two-legged creatures generally content themselves with the title'.[49] Locke had never contented himself with titles alone, and when he died, on 28 October 1704, in the company of his closest friend and companion Damaris Masham, his reputation as a major, if extremely controversial, philosopher had been firmly established, both in England and on the Continent. His contractual

political theory would continue to win the accolades of some Whig
politicians on both sides of the Atlantic throughout the next century,
his pioneering exploration of the limits of knowledge would inform
most subsequent British philosophical inquiry, and his religious speculation would continue to inspire both those who would separate
religious convictions from civil rights and those who would brave
accusations of heterodoxy in defence of the right to personal exegesis.

Locke's life of counsel has been brought into sharp relief over the
past ten years with the publication of E.S. De Beer's magisterial
edition of the philosopher's correspondence, now complete in eight
volumes. No other source gives us such a rich and detailed picture of
Locke's intellectual curiosity and broad range of interests. His many
letters to friends in Holland, especially letters to Limborch and to
Furly, reveal the depth of his concern with religious questions, and of
his own efforts to make some contribution to the eradication of
intolerance, to set people on the path of personal inquiry without
hindrance from external authorities. Letters to Edward Clarke, to
Clarke's wife Mary, and to their children, communicate his intense
interest in education as the agency for creating the moral person. The
letters to Damaris Masham speak to, among other things, the poverty
of Locke's aesthetic and poetic sensibility, his distrust of the imagination, his overriding concern for the practical, even in religion. Correspondence with scientific figures, including fellow physicians, offers
abundant insight into the nature of the investigatory process at a
moment when the English scientific community was embracing the
empirical method advocated by Locke.

The importance of friendship for the bachelor-philosopher, for
regular communication with those who sympathized with his positions, elucidates how strongly Locke, who understood the novel nature
of much of his work, relied upon the intellectual support of others.
Perhaps no exchange was as important in this respect as that which
took place between Locke and the Deist Anthony Collins during the
final year of the philosopher's life. Collins was 27 when Locke first
encountered him; he immediately accepted the young man's effusive
praise for his philosophical work as a sure sign of a discriminating and
worthwhile critic. In a sense, if a letter Locke wrote to his cousin Peter
King about Collins is an adequate reflection of the philosopher's mind
at this late juncture, Collins was a symbol of hope for the successful
transmission of Locke's ideas to a new generation and a new century.
And to Collins he confessed that were he again a young man just
setting out on the pilgrimage of earthly tenure, 'I shoud think it my

great happiness to have such a companion as you, who had a relish of truth. . .and, if I mistake not you have as much of it as I ever met with in anybody.'[50] Truth in the company of like minds, the search for the limits of human knowledge and the formulation of a life plan based upon those limitations, such had been the larger enterprise from the early days at Christ Church. That the conclusion of the enterprise for the man John Locke should occur at the outset of the *siècle des lumières* was not without its special symmetry.

2
KNOWLEDGE, DUTY, AND SALVATION

The immediate occasion for Locke's greatest work, *An Essay Concerning Human Understanding* (1689), was a discussion amongst a small circle of friends over questions of morality and religion, those parts of knowledge, he tells the reader, 'that Men are most concern'd to be clear in'. Before the group could proceed to investigate theological and moral questions, however, it was thought necessary to step back and see what our abilities were and how far they extended. Locke undertook to provide the requisite preliminaries, doubtless unaware that the overall task would engage him for the next 18 years. These early meetings probably took place sometime in 1670 or 1671 at Anthony Ashley Cooper's London home, for by the close of 1671 Locke had completed two drafts of what would eventually emerge as the *Essay*.[1] There are additional comments sprinkled throughout the published work which seem to indicate that Locke wished to address concerns about normative conduct and theology broadly defined, and it is worth keeping in mind that his inquiries began after he had broken with the Church of England's position on the evil of toleration – and after the failed effort by the latitudinarians to achieve a comprehension in 1668. However short our knowledge may prove to be, all humans 'have Light enough to lead them to a Knowledge of their Maker, and the sight of their own Duties' was how he phrased it at the opening of Book 1, while in the fourth Book he reminded his audience 'that our proper Imployment lies in those Enquiries, and in that sort of Knowledge, which is most suited to our natural Capacities, and carries in it our greatest interest, i.e. the Condition of our eternal Estate'.[2]

When Locke mentioned 'our natural Capacities' he was speaking in
reference to a contemporary and commonplace view of creation where
every living thing enjoys an assigned station in the vast sweep of
nature. A great order of creation embracing all ranks of creatures had
been set upon the earth by a benevolent designer, and each being was
distinguished by particular attributes special to its God-given nature.
Genesis 1.26 and Psalms 115.16 had established humankind's pre-
eminent station on earth with mastery linked to the gift of reason, and
Locke found no reason to demur from this ancient position. It seems
fair to suggest that the little group that gathered in Locke's rooms was
interested in discovering how one arrives at principles of morality, the
means by which universal moral rules, those firm guideposts regulating
one's duty to God, are made known. It was a problem of immediate
import, for by the 1670s the re-established Church of England had
clearly not succeeded in extinguishing dissent through state-sponsored
persecution. A considerable minority of the population continued to
embrace alternative visions of the godly community where moral
precepts found their articulation and endorsement outside a hierarchically organized and authoritarian Church establishment.

The failure of coercion, however, was by no means due to lack of
effort on the part of the High Church episcopacy and its numerous and
powerful parliamentary backers. It has been made abundantly clear
by scholars over the last decade that the Church of England was not
an institution in terminal decline during the late seventeenth century.[3]
The vehemence of radical polemic against the Church's political
influence is alone sound evidence of the vigour of the clerical edifice.
Retaining both its social and its considerable political power after the
return of Charles II, the Church claimed a monopoly over theological
and moral discipline. It alone enjoyed sacerdotal or priestly powers to
perform sacrificial functions and to exercise supernatural powers on
behalf of the laity; it alone was empowered to set sanctions for the
violation of the innate and immutable laws of Christian ethics. The
basis of the Church's claim to power rested with its self-definition as
the sole institutional conduit of divine grace; it was a supernatural, not
a man-made entity, and saving grace was unavailable outside its
doors. In the minds of apologists for the Church, separation meant
schism, and schism resulted in damnation.[4] From birth to death the
journey of life was enveloped by the many features of the religious year
– festivals, holy days, prayers, communion – all organized and
supervised by the episcopally ordained priest whose pulpit was the
primary vehicle for the transmission of everything from news of the

mundane to directives concerning appropriate Christian conduct and belief. The implication, at least, behind the Clarendon Code, was that the Anglican priesthood enjoyed a monopoly over the truths that mattered, over genuine and life-saving knowledge.

Locke's inquiry in the *Essay*, then, was not merely an epistemic exercise removed from the major issues of his day, for in its bold assertion that all humans proceeded from God's hands with the same faculties, it also very directly called into question the social position and political prerogatives of the *jure divino* Church of England. It was, of course, a book concerned with the nature, the origins, of knowledge and true religion, but by omitting any direct discussion of the Church's monopolistic claims, in declaring that God's image had been imparted to all persons indiscriminately, Locke was challenging the very competence of the English – and by inference the European – confessional state. He would remain a communicant in the Church of England throughout his life, and while he felt that his Church was gifted with preachers 'whose lives as well as sermons I looke upon and verily believe, to be the most seriously Christian that are now in the world or have bin at any time in the Church',[5] he abstained from conceding to any church exclusive wisdom respecting the divine ordinances for humankind.

More broadly speaking, Locke and other observers were keenly aware that a larger 'rule of faith' controversy had stood at the centre of Europe's religious and military conflicts over the previous 150 years, and that a proper elucidation of the foundations of knowledge and belief might serve to ameliorate some of the friction between rival parties. In 1677, during the course of his extended visit to France, Locke had written in his journal that mankind's major task centred on discovering 'what law he is to live by here and still be jugd by hereafter', assuming always that one set of guidelines, one natural law, was what God intended for humankind.[6] By first discovering the source and limits of knowledge, by enquiring 'into the Original, Certainty, and Extent of humane Knowledge; together, with the Grounds and Degrees of Belief, Opinion, and Assent', one could, it was hoped, begin to make supportable statements about the possibility of creating a science of morality, universally acceptable norms of human conduct, and the grounds of legitimate civil authority, all essential preliminaries to anyone interested in securing the gift of Christian salvation.[7]

Locke had actually begun his investigations into the rules which ought to guide human conduct and the nature of our access to those rules while he was a young lecturer at Christ Church in the early 1660s. Not published until the 1950s, these *Essays on the Law of Nature* attend to four pretended sources of human knowledge: inscription, tradition, sense experience, and Revelation. Arguments for inscription, he wrote at the time, were belied by the fact that so few people agreed on common practical (moral) and speculative principles. This theme was later at the heart of the first of the four Books which comprise the *Essay*. Proponents of tradition as a source of knowledge were hard pressed to address the uncomfortable fact that belief and behavioural norms varied widely from one society to the next. Revelation was for Locke a legitimate source of moral knowledge, but since it could not be acquired through natural means, it could not be considered the result of man's independent intellectual efforts. Experience or the observation of particulars, on the other hand, offered a plausible and even compelling basis for knowledge because it finds its anchor in God's creative intentions and in man's active intellect.[8] A benevolent Creator had provided humankind with the requisite mental abilities to work upon the data of sense and arrive at the law of nature without reference to tradition or human authority. The central claim of these early academic lectures, then, was that reasonable men could know the contents of natural law and recognize its binding character. This is the position that would develop over the years before finding its final voice in the *Essay*.

The *Essay* was a controversial work which immediately enjoyed a wide readership. Locke supervised four editions before his death in 1704, and he began further revisions on a fifth edition which appeared in 1706. The book, which was written in a plain style and where references to learned authorities were kept to a minimum, was intended for a non-specialist audience, not for philosophers and theologians. In fact the author made no apologies in the event that 'the speculative and quick-sighted should complain of my being in some parts tedious, than that any one, not accustomed to abstract Speculations, or prepossessed with different Notions, should mistake, or not comprehend my meaning'.[9] Locke hoped that the book would provide practical advice to men of affairs on the conduct of their lives, and in their preparation for eternal happiness. But criticism of the work was almost immediate, beginning soon after the publication of an abridgment in the January 1688 issue of Jean Le Clerc's *Bibliothèque Universelle*. Like so much of the publishing of the seventeenth century, the criticism was of a polemical nature, written in order to respond to what were thought to be dangerous doctrines. As we have seen in the previous chapter, Locke answered very few of his detractors in the years after publication, finding little merit in most of the attacks, and preferring instead to engage in amicable correspondence with friends who had nothing but undiluted praise for his efforts.

The *Essay* adopts a very hostile view of traditional scholastic learning, embracing instead the ideal of discourse utilized by the proponents of the new science in the Royal Society. Disputations, which were still key to the university curriculum, and where graduation depended upon a successful performance in debate, represented all that was wrong with a word-bound form of learning. Like Francis Bacon, Thomas Sprat, and even Robert Boyle before him, Locke thought that while the maxims of the schools were useful for silencing an opponent in debate, they did little to advance genuine knowledge, and nothing to fashion conduct. The confrontational style of the disputation illustrated the arrogance, the hollowness of a system that assumed expansive boundaries for human knowledge. In the *Essay*, true knowledge for Locke was much more limited than scholasticism would admit.[10] But the reduction of authentic knowledge to a sphere more befitting a finite creature whose main task was moral reform in pursuit of divine reward in no respect detracted from man's dignity or prominence of place in God's universe. In fact what we can know – duties to each other and to God – turns out to be what is most important for our future prospects. Locke's self-described 'under-labourer' image, where the task at hand is 'clearing the ground a little and removing some of the rubbish that lies in the way to knowledge' set the stage for an attack on traditional, and to Locke's mind, unexamined theories of knowledge where pretension took the place of introspection and careful observation, where the abuse of words so common to the schoolmen turned discussion into babel.[11] Locke would explore how the mind works, its ability to assemble, compare, compound and abstract ideas, following the new and more productive rules of observation and attention outlined and prescribed by the virtuosi of the Royal Society.[12]

The well-known Lockean assault upon innate ideas contained in Book 1 of the *Essay* was a pointed response to religious and moral problems much under discussion in the seventeenth century. The religious conflicts of the sixteenth and seventeenth centuries had claimed thousands of innocent lives in bloody struggles to define an appropriate rule of faith or guide in matters related to the most important business in life: eternal salvation. Claimants to authority were constantly challenged by an advancing scepticism which called into question existing bodies of knowledge that had long supported traditional structures of authority in church and state. Most moralists and theologians during Locke's lifetime maintained that innate knowledge, particularly innate practical knowledge (knowledge of moral principles) was essential to the stability of the established moral and religious order. Some variant of the theory of innate ideas, according to John Yolton, 'can be found in almost any pamphlet of the early part of the century dealing with morality, conscience, the existence of God, or natural law'.[13] For Locke, these widespread appeals to innate ideas, or innate dispositions which predispose us to the good – appeals not unlike the assertion of Thomas Aquinas that men share in the divine reason 'from which they derive a natural inclination to such actions and ends as are fitting' – countenanced intellectual laziness and stood in opposition to the more critical experiential emphasis so popular in the new scientific culture.[14] This culture emphasized research and experiment, movement from the particular to the general. For Locke it was a non-dispositional power of judgement working on the data provided by sensory evidence that marked the road to certainty.

Recently James Tully has argued that Locke's polemic against innate knowledge was of a piece with his wider attack on authoritarianism in religion, science, and politics across Europe. Innatism, with its teleological emphasis upon man's natural inclination toward what is right, was for Locke the epistemological equivalent of the medieval cosmology where purpose and striving explain the motion of heavenly bodies.[15] In addition, religious elites, Protestant and Catholic alike, commonly used the innatist hypothesis in order to appropriate power for themselves and to suppress all voices of dissent. The *Essay* challenged every regime of knowledge and belief formation where it was assumed that the mind was naturally disposed to the true and the good. Locke had little patience for those who would perpetuate existing structures of authority by the appeal to innatism. As he stated bluntly in the first Book: 'it was of no small advantage to those who affected to be Masters and Teachers, to make this the Principle of Principles, That Principles must not be questioned.'[16] Once it is accepted that some doctrines are beyond dispute, as soon as an examination of certain cherished principles is excluded, the road to arbitrary government by self-interested elites is thrown open. 'Nor is it a small power it gives one man over another, to have the Authority to be the Dictator of Principles, and Teacher of unquestionable Truths; and to make a Man swallow that for an innate Principle, which may serve to his purpose, who teacheth them.'[17] And if amongst those

unquestioned principles was the duty to take up arms against people
who held contradictory religious beliefs, then so much the worse for
Europe. Not the least of the goals of the *Essay* was to sweep away the
epistemological foundations of the *ancien régime* in Europe, establishing
in its place the twin powers of custom and education in shaping
thought and action. Achieving this goal would result in nothing less
than a nullification of the hierarchical paradigm which had defined
the relationship between subject and superior in political and religious
life since the earliest Christian era.

One of the most common arguments employed by proponents of
innate knowledge during Locke's day was based on the appeal to
universal assent, the claim that all people, despite minor variations,
endorse a set of generally similar moral precepts. Theologians in
particular were eager to maintain that every generation accepted,
without reflection, certain basic moral axioms regardless of cultural
differences – that murder is wrong, that covenants should be honoured, that honesty in personal relations should be respected, and that
God should be obeyed – such rules as these could not be denied by
creatures endowed by God with reasonable and immortal souls.
Thomas Burnet, in a letter of 1697 to the author of the *Essay*, stated
that 'the Distinction, suppose of Gratitude and Ingratitude, Fidelity
and Infidelity, Justice and Injustice, and such others, is as sudden
without any Ratiocination. . . 'Tis not like a Theorem, which we come
to know by the help of precedent Demonstrations and Postulatums,
but it rises as quick as any of our Passions, or as Laughter at the sight
of a ridiculous Accident or Object.'[18] Locke went to some trouble in
Book 1 of the *Essay* to provide examples of persons, such as children,
who did not accept current Christian notions of morality as a matter of
course, but more importantly, he insisted that if the doctrine of innate
ideas were accepted, it would make all further instruction in the
principles of morality a redundant exercise. Men would know and
act upon their fundamental moral obligations without previous direction. As one important proponent of innate ideas, Nathaniel Culverwell, stated in his *Elegant and Learned Discourse of the Light of Nature*
(1654): 'There are stampt and printed upon the being of man, some
cleare and undelible Principles, some first and Alphabetical Notions;
by putting together of which it can spell out the Law of Nature.'[19] And
yet for Locke it was obvious that the purported existence of innate
practical principles had done little to dispel the religious tensions of
seventeenth-century Europe; people clearly had a variety of conflicting
notions concerning the law of nature and its primary obligations. For

the Quaker, God's law as revealed by the 'inner light' called for a rejection of the oaths which held civil society together, while for the Puritan saint that same law had legitimized the overthrow and execution of the monarch in 1649; for the Catholic recusant the dictate of the pope was the expression of the divine word, and for the Deist of the 1690s the eternal law was synonymous with the mandate of human reason, thereby making Revelation dispensable. Having observed the unhappy results of some of these disparate opinions in the religious and political turmoil of his youth, Locke concluded wryly 'that if different Men of different Sects should go about to give us a list of those innate practical Principles, they would set down only such as suited their distinct Hypotheses, and were fit to support the Doctrines of their particular Schools or Churches'.[20] While Locke at this point in his life did not doubt the existence of a knowable law of nature which is binding upon all persons, his own commonsense, observational approach to current theories of knowledge forced him to suspect an epistemology so clearly at odds with daily experience. Even the traditional reliance upon conscience as a special telic faculty naturally disposed toward the true and the good and a break upon immoral actions was rejected by Locke, thanks mainly to the subjectivity of radical sectaries during the Interregnum who claimed 'the god within' for their actions. As early as 1660, in a decisive break with the conventional interpretation of St Paul's dictum in Romans 2.14–15, where the law which the Gentiles follow is 'written in their hearts', Locke described pretended conscience as little more than an opinion of the truth of a proposition, and in the *Essay* it was equated with 'our own Opinion or Judgment of the Moral Rectitude or Pravity of our own Actions'.[21]

The new Lockean basis for knowledge and certainty, the original of all ideas and ultimately the ground of all assent which so disturbed his contemporaries, was addressed in Book 2 of the *Essay*, the first of three Books where Locke presents his constructive argument. 'Our Observation', he wrote, 'employed either about external, sensible Objects; or about the internal Operations of our Minds, perceived and reflected on by our selves, is that, which supplies our Understandings with all the materials of thinking.'[22] All we know is from sensation and reflection upon the objects of sensation, a simple position which in one stroke erased the claims of all existing structures of authority in religion, science, and politics. Outward sense and inward perception; beyond these two basic sources we could know nothing. But the simple assembling of ideas from experience was not synonymous with knowl-

edge for Locke; rather he argued that the mind had to first establish
relations between its store of ideas, a process which is either immediate
(intuitive) or demonstrative, the latter requiring the intervention of
intermediate ideas before a connection between two principal ideas
can be established. His discussion of errors in the acquisition of
knowledge through the misuse of words, the improper association of
ideas, and faulty demonstration, all contributed to the overall message
respecting man's limited nature. And where intuition and demonstration failed us, in that wide area where knowledge was not to be
secured, we were obliged to fall back on probability or assent based
upon the best evidence available to us.

Because human knowledge is so sharply circumscribed, probability
becomes our chief guide in daily actions, informing everything from
historical investigations and business engagements to judicial testimony and questions of evidence.[23] Indeed 'most of the Propositions we
think, reason, discourse, nay act upon, are such, as we cannot have
undoubted Knowledge of their Truth'. We believe or assent to
propositions which lack certainty because probability is 'suitable. . .to
that State of Mediocrity and Probationship, he [God] has been pleased
to place us in here'.[24] Ultimately it was this discovery of the limitations
of our knowledge and the uncertain nature of probable belief that led
Locke to consistently reaffirm the propriety of a broad toleration in his
own country. Instead of extending the parameters of human cogni-
zance in a manner appropriate to the emerging spirit of enlightened
rationalism characteristic of the eighteenth century, Locke pointedly
compressed both our ability to know and our potential for securing less
than certainty when knowledge eludes us. Still, as he announced
in the introduction, God has bestowed upon humankind powers well
above the rest of creation. 'We shall not have much Reason to
complain of the narrowness of our Minds', he said, 'if we will but
employ them about what may be of use to us.' And what was useful in
the end concerned not the body but the soul, not a mastery of nature
but the regulation of the inner self, not the terrene but the transcendent. According to Locke, 'methinks they have a low Opinion of their
Souls, who lay out all of their Incomes in Provisions for the Body'.[25]
The anti-authoritarian temper of the *Essay* did not mean that Locke
was eager to champion notions of human self-sufficiency in the broader
project at the heart of his philosophy: self-discipline and the mastery of
base desires prerequisite to the discovery of the law which, if adhered
to as scrupulously as human frailty allowed, would guide us to
salvation.

One of the most controversial aspects of the *Essay*, and the one that had the most serious implications for the prevailing metaphysics, involved Locke's insistence that the external world was not appre- hended directly by the understanding, but that ideas alone make up the raw material of our knowledge. According to the epistemology of the *Essay*, we are acquainted with ideas alone, a cognitive and not a physical reality, and knowledge emerges solely out of the varied relationships of these ideas. Defining knowledge as 'the perception of the connection and agreement, or disagreement and repugnancy of any of our Ideas', this separation of the 'thing-in-itself' from the product of perception seemed to open the door to a form of scepticism where the underlying substance of matter, indeed a world of physical objects itself, was no longer certain. ''Tis evident', he continued, 'the Mind knows not Things immediately, but only by the intervention of the Ideas it has of them.'[26] In the opinion of his sharpest critics, Locke's new 'way of ideas' removed the possibility of knowing God's handiwork on its own terms, or in its real nature. Humans were now restricted to a subjective mental world of their own creation. And the ideas formed by individuals varied widely. As Locke himself asked his readers, 'Is there any thing so extravagant, as the Imaginations of Men's Brains? Where is the Head that has no Chimeras in it?' What possible criteria were available to distinguish between the clear and distinct (but false) ideas of the religious enthusiast, for example, 'and the Reasonings of a sober Man'?[27] If the madman could intuit a clear relationship between what others thought to be unrelated ideas, upon what grounds could the majority gainsay the madman his truth?

The epistemology of the *Essay* clearly reflected the changing con- ception of science in the seventeenth century. Henry More had earlier raised doubts about our ability to discover the essence of substance, while Locke's friends Robert Boyle and Isaac Newton, among others, found themselves at odds with the conventional view that the task of science was to gain knowledge of the real, inner essence of things.[28] For the members of the Royal Society, empirical investigations into nature yielded knowledge of the phenomenal properties of corporeal sub- stance leading to the ability to predict nature's course, but these investigations offered nothing regarding the essence of substance underlying appearance, the corpuscular structure. The new science did not concern itself with the insensible parts of nature on which all its other properties depend. In this crucial respect, the results of all empirical investigations were subject to doubt pending future evidence.[29] Locke's *Essay*, then, helped to provide the philosophical underpinnings of the new science, where interest in substantial forms gave way to a description of experienced nature.

And yet while Locke understood that knowledge of substance might elude human powers, he saw that it was knowledge of things that gave preference to one person's ideas over another's, to the ideas of the majority over the clear and distinct ideas of the madman in the case mentioned above. Anticipating the criticism of his 'way of ideas' for established metaphysical theory, he concluded that there were two sorts of ideas which agree with objects in nature. The first were simple ideas produced by things in nature 'operating on the Mind in a natural way'. Although he could not say how thought could be caused by physical processes, he maintained that simple ideas 'are not fictions of our Fancies, but the natural and regular productions of Things without us' and these ideas represent the things in nature to us in a manner and form consistent with God's intentions for humankind. The second category, and the central one in terms of establishing a science of morality, involved all complex ideas, excluding those of substance for which our ideas were imperfect. Complex ideas were formed by the mind's ability to combine several simple ideas originating in sensation or reflection.[30] According to Locke some of these complex ideas–which he called modes – were not copies of anything existing outside us in nature, thus it was possible to secure real knowledge in this area by carefully defining what we meant by each of these ideas. Mathematics is one example he used in this context. No one doubts the existence of mathematical truths, and yet the student 'considers the Truth and Properties belonging to a Rectangle, or Circle, only as they are in Idea in his own Mind. For ' 'tis possible he never found either of them existing mathematically, i.e. precisely true, in his Life'.[31] Following this argument, Locke moves on to consider how moral knowledge is capable of certainty, how we might establish a true science of human conduct that meets the requirements of the law of nature or God's eternal dictate for humankind.

In Book 4 of the *Essay* he stated clearly that 'Morality is the proper Science, and Business of Mankind in general', a position that reaffirmed his fundamental disengagement from the predominantly temporal concerns of the Enlightenment. And he was confident that given the requisite intellectual application 'Morality is capable of Demonstration, as well as Mathematics. . .' Demonstrative knowledge required the employment of the mind's various powers – discernment, comparing, abstracting and composing complex ideas from simple ones – but the task was not an insuperable one. 'This knowledge by intervening Proofs, though it be certain, yet the evidence of it is not altogether so clear and bright, nor the assent so ready, as in intuitive Knowledge. For though in Demonstration, the Mind does at last perceive the Agreement or Disagreement of the Ideas it considers; yet 'tis not without pains and attention.'[32] As we have noticed, his confidence in our ability to secure knowledge of universal moral principles was based largely on the fact that moral ideas, like mathematical terms, and unlike ideas of objects in nature, have no archetypes outside the mind itself. People may carefully attach precise definitions to words used to signify moral ideas because there are no external referents or facts to which the moral ideas must conform. Acts of injustice or benevolence, for example, must fit the definitions which we have formulated using our language. We can apprehend moral ideas perfectly so long as we agree upon definitions with other persons. 'For the Ideas that Ethicks are conversant about, being all real Essences, and such as, I imagine, have a discoverable connection and agreement one with another; so far as we can find their Habitudes and Relations, so far we shall be possessed of certain, real, and general Truths.' The job of creating this science of morality would not be successful if 'Vices, Passions, and domineering Interests' interfered with the work of discovery, but if individuals took the time to consider the idea of a God who is infinite in power and goodness, who has created mankind and made him an understanding, reasonable being, then Locke expressed the hope that 'the measures of right and wrong might be made out', affording unerring direction in the search for salvation.[33]

As a committed Christian, Locke believed that the source and executor of morality is a God 'who sees Men in the dark, has in his Hand Rewards and Punishments, and Power enough to call to account the Proudest Offender'. The accounting, Locke assumed, would take place in a life after this one. Morality is not about a set of arid definitions or conceptual connections arbitrarily fashioned by a particular society, but a much broader code whose origin is founded in the eternal law or the law of nature. Moral good and evil are determined by 'the Conformity or Disagreement of our voluntary Actions to some Law, whereby Good and Evil is drawn on us, from the Will and Power of the Law-maker'.[34] This was, of course, a widely held view in the seventeenth century, one certainly embraced by members of the official and dissenting churches. Unlike his Calvinist forebears, Locke saw no tension between basing the law of nature on the will of God and

the requirements of reason, for both, in Locke's mind, were synonymous. Locke sharply criticized ancient moralists who made earthly
reputation and reward the final guarantor of a temporal moral order,
insisting that stronger sanctions were necessary to motivate individuals
into compliance with the discoverable law of nature. As he made clear
in the *Essay*, it would not be enough simply to establish the reasonable
(and thus God-ordained) nature of behaving in a particular manner;
men must be threatened with divine punishment and lured by the
promise of eternal happiness before they will accede to the voice of
reason.

The many difficulties involved in attempting to motivate people to
follow universal moral rules, to make them see that adherence to the
law of nature is in their best interest and conducive to the greatest
personal happiness, highlights Locke's traditional Christian estimate of
human nature and human potential. He believed that while people
were endowed by a loving Creator 'with a power to suspend any
particular desire' until we have investigated 'the good or evil of what
we are going to do', this defence of human freedom did not ignore the
more difficult fact that few men appeared to obey the moral law in
their daily affairs. In the first edition of the *Essay*, Locke had adopted
what is known as an 'intellectualist' approach to the question of what
determined the will. How one behaves in the moral arena, Locke had
concluded, is determined by what one believes is right and wrong. Bad
actions, sinful actions, are the result of faulty intellect, some cognitive
defect. William Molyneux gently took issue with this intellectualist
approach here when he wrote to Locke suggesting that 'it seems harsh
to say, that a Man shall be Damn'd, because he understands no better
than he does'.[35] Unwilling to accept the implications of such an
approach for what it implied about the character of a supposedly
benevolent God, Locke re-evaluated and then reversed his position,
introducing what one scholar has referred to as 'the non-intellectual
roots of action'.[36]

Beginning with his additions to the 1694 second edition of the *Essay*,
Locke stated that throughout most of their lives people were motivated
solely by what was thought to be in the interest of their immediate,
and not their eternal, happiness. The greatest good, even if acknowledged, 'does not determine the will, until our desire, raised propor-
tionable to it, makes us uneasy in the want of it'. And raising that
desire, creating an environment where persons, in the words of St
Matthew, 'hunger and thirst after righteousness', was no simple task,
and certainly not one to be achieved through the voice of unassisted

reason. Reasonable people will see the greater good and acknowledge it to be such, but present uneasiness will more often than not determine their will. 'How many are to be found, that have had lively representations set before their minds of the unspeakable joys of Heaven, which they acknowledge both possible and probable too, who yet would be content to take up with their happiness here?' Building a demonstrative system of morality, then, was simply one part of a much larger overall task; supernatural sanctions and a redirection of one's will were obviously necessary if the dictate of reason were to have any appreciable impact on the lives of humankind. Regrettably, the 'Principles of Action' that are lodged in our appetites, if not somehow restrained by important sanctions, 'would carry Men to the overturning of all Morality'.[37] It would become the job of the educator to ensure that morality was not overturned, that the free agent suspended action and considered the requirements of God's will.

Locke's theory here, what amounted to a hedonistic Christian ethics, was widely shared by his friends and contemporaries in the Church of England, men whose theology was anchored in centuries-old assumptions about mankind's corrupt nature. Even the most sanguine observer of the human condition could not help but observe the total failure of moral codes, even those which enjoyed the enforcement power of civil authorities. As the latitudinarian Archbishop of Canterbury John Tillotson observed, men have lost 'in good measure, the love and relish of true happiness', and only fear, the threat of eternal torments, would convince them to practise a living faith with any consistency. Fear, he admitted, 'being as intimate to our natures, it is the strongest bond of laws, and the great security of our duty'.[38] A potential science of morality built upon the foundation of reason and the clearly defined terms which stood as their own archetypes offered little comfort to those who, like Locke, found the religious disagreements of the Restoration period injurious to the immediate task of individual reform before a God who sees men in the dark and will judge them according to their actions and not on the basis of their particular beliefs.

Locke never did fulfil the wishes and importunities of friends to build a demonstrative morality whereby specific duties are discovered to follow from moral relations.[39] The *Essay* did not provide its readers with the specific contents of the law of nature or God's law drawn from reason. Nor did it explain in anything approaching adequate detail how reasonable men could arrive at a universally applicable natural law. The more optimistic implications of the *Essay* were not to be pursued with any consistency or application. Indeed towards the end of his life, in *A Paraphrase and Notes on the Epistles of St. Paul*, Locke confessed that there appeared to be no clearly established moral law aside from the revealed law, a relatively late historical development. Specifically, in a note on Romans 2.14, he claimed that 'from Adam to Christ there was noe revealed positive law but that given to the Israelites'.[40] In the end he recommended an alternative source of unshakable moral precepts, a source at once easily accessible and widely commended. In a paper titled 'Of Ethick in General' which Locke seems to have intended for a chapter in the *Essay*, he stated that the true measure of morality was to be found 'in the commands of the great God of heaven and earth, and such as according to which he would retribute to men after this life'.[41] The morality of the Gospel so far exceeds the cogency of any other source, he advised in 'Some Thoughts concerning Reading and Study for a Gentleman', 'that to give a man a ful knowledge of true Morality, I should send him to no other Book, but the New Testament'.[42] Determining the parameters of God's intentions and the specific content of natural law required a return to Scripture, an endorsement hardly reflective of the claims put forward in the *Essay*, but one which the majority of Locke's readers could accept without qualification.

In 1695, with the publication of *The Reasonableness of Christianity*, Locke offered his contemporaries a simple exegesis of the New Testament that highlighted the moral teachings of Jesus, cleansing these eternal precepts 'from the corrupt glosses of the Scribes and Pharisees'. Locke wrote, in a manner at odds with the more hopeful tone of the *Essay*, that natural religion had never been established through the application of reason alone. 'It should seem', he confessed, 'that it is too hard a task for unassisted reason to establish morality in all its parts, upon its true foundation, with a clear and convincing light.'[43] It seemed more efficacious, at least 'to the apprehensions of the vulgar, and mass of mankind' that a morality sent directly from God serve in lieu of one potentially discovered by reason, especially since to date 'human reason unassisted failed men in its great and proper business of morality. It never from unquestionable principles, by clear deductions, made out an entire body of the law of nature.'[44] Specific moral rules consistent with the pursuit of eternal happiness were readily available to all due to the simple generosity of the Creator.

Locke's reluctance to undertake the project for a demonstrable morality, to tread where eminent pagan philosophers had worked and failed, and where their Christian successors had been able to do little beyond glossing the rules contained in Scripture, was made easier by the fact that the truths of Revelation, 'as soon as they are heard and considered, they are found to be agreeable to reason'. Christ was the first to assemble an unerring rule of conduct, and the obligation to follow the rule flowed from the nature of his mission to save a sinful humanity. In the *Reasonableness*, Locke stated that we do ourselves no service in attributing the failure of our unassisted efforts to negligence, a point central to the discussion on the topic in the *Essay*. The truth now was that 'our Saviour found mankind under a corruption of manners and principles, which ages after ages had prevailed, and must be confessed, was not in a way or tendency to be mended'.[45] Without the gratuitous addition of sacred Revelation during and after Christ's lifetime, the prospects for a significant reform of conduct, and more importantly for eternal salvation, were something less than propitious.

Locke's return to Scripture as our only dependable source for instruction in principles of morality congruent with the divine law of nature placed him squarely within a rich and ancient Christian tradition. At the core of that tradition was the notion of faith as a legitimate and supportive epistemic category, one clearly beyond the parameters of normal sense experience. Locke used the word faith in two separate contexts. Throughout most of the *Essay* he equated faith with assent to propositions which we accept even though we do not have certain knowledge of their truth. In this context he associated faith with opinion, assent, or belief given after critical examination of the proposal in question.[46] The second use of the word involves its more familiar religious connotation. Here faith is assent to Revelation which is synonymous with assurance beyond the least doubt. Individuals might just as soon doubt their own being as to question whether Revelation is the direct word of God. In the *Essay* he defined this second type of faith as 'the Assent to any Proposition, not thus made out by the Deductions of Reason; but upon the Credit of the Proposer, as coming from God, in some extraordinary way of Communication'.[47] Of course one had to be sure that the Revelation was in fact from God and not simply the fancy of the individual's imagination, but once the credentials of the messenger were established, faith in a theological sense became a principal guide to human action. And reason – mankind's most precious divine gift – would be employed to determine the authenticity of the source.[48] Here Locke would follow the advice of his elder acquaintance Benjamin Whichcote, who said 'We are not to submit our Understanding to the belief of these things, that are contrary to our Understanding. We must have a Reason, for that which we believe above our Reason.'[49] Following this rule, Locke believed that we would not be misled in the manner of the enthusiast who takes his own fancy or imagination for the directive of God. In the fourth edition of the *Essay* (1700), he added a chapter 'Of Enthusiasm' which, despite its almost personal venom, in a sense sums up the entire spirit of the Restoration Church of England with respect to the uses of intuition and emotion. He was certainly not the first to criticize the proponents of personalized, trans-rational communication with God. While Locke was still a student at Christ Church the Cambridge Platonist Henry More had equated enthusiasm with atheism in the sense that both were born of 'an overbearing Phancy'. Locke's hostility toward anyone who believed that they alone enjoyed the particular favour of the divine was built upon the memory of civil war sectarianism and its unverifiable criterion for legitimate authority. For Locke, faith had to be built upon a foundation of reason lest the excesses of the European-wide wars of religion recur. Enthusiasm in religion is a constant danger because it is so attractive to the conceited and lazy intellect, it excuses one from 'the tedious and not always successful Labour of strict Reasoning'. Even good men occasionally fall prey to the appeal of immediate (and erroneous) inspiration: St Paul's persecution of his Christian neighbours was the example with the most resonance for Locke.[50]

In discovering the parameters of our duty before a God who on the last day will judge according to actions in this life, Locke felt obliged to make a distinction between 'man' and 'person'. The former was the biological organism where particles of matter succeed each other within the same body. Everyone begins life as a mere organism; personhood is reached once the individual elevates himself through education to a point where he appropriates and recognizes actions as his own, taking responsibility for those actions as a moral being. Person is then 'a Forensick Term appropriating Actions and their Merit' where the consequences of actions are immediately accepted by the agent who sees himself as God's special handiwork. The distinction between man and person was an important one because without awareness and ownership of actions, the man cannot be held responsible for breaches of the natural law set as the standard for humankind by his Maker. Praise and blame – or eternal reward or punishment – can only be affixed to a person who recognizes and acknowledges specific actions as his own; it is this recognition alone that constitutes personal identity. The eschatological implications of this position are unmistakable: on the last day sentencing 'shall be justified by the consciousness all Persons shall have, that they themselves in what Bodies soever they appear, or what Substances soever that consciousness adheres to, are the *same*, that committed those Actions, and deserve that Punishment for them'.[51]

In calling into question the legitimacy of structures of knowledge based upon putative innate ideas, then, Locke was placing himself at odds with established power elites in church and state whose basis of authority could be traced in large measure to the influence of arbitrary and manufactured tradition. It was the uncritical acceptance of these deliberately formulated bodies of knowledge that Locke took exception to, patterns of thought and behaviour that had been responsible for so much of the political and religious instability of his own century. Encouraging intellectual lassitude and moral irresponsibility, defenders of the religious and political status quo would have Englishmen continue in their fruitless – and ultimately unchristian – attempts to stamp out dissent before alternative positions receive a fair hearing. Locke challenged his contemporaries to reconstruct knowledge from what he took to be its only legitimate foundation in experience, and he cautioned that one of the results of this natural rebuilding would be the surprising restriction of knowledge to within a short compass. The familiar scholastic pretensions to mastery over mind and matter had to be abandoned in favour of knowledge sufficient for frail creatures seeking an end to change and decay through the unmerited favour of their saviour.

In accepting the narrow purview of knowledge, in recognizing the potential for one to err when relying upon probability in daily thought and action, in reluctantly admitting that the entire law of nature had never been made out by the force of unassisted reason, and in confirming that his ethical theory provided small hope that men would act in accordance with the law even if it were established in full by reason, Locke was obliged – in fact he was eager – to shift his attention to an alternative source of moral order and obligation. That source, one might claim, appeared in certain respects to return to a traditional authority structure, but in fact Locke approached Scripture with the same critical sense that guided his evaluation of knowledge derived from sensation and reflection. God's rule of conduct for his creatures – if it is to be treated as genuine – must conform to the unchanging rule of reason. Revelation will not be contrary to our clear intuitive knowledge because a good God would not overthrow the requirements of the one faculty which distinguished humanity from the rest of creation. That some angels rebelled, that the dead shall awaken on the last day, that persons shall live for eternity after judgement: these tenets may be above the reach of knowledge anchored in experience, but none of them defies the framework of rationality.

Building the basis of knowledge anew in late seventeenth-century England meant nothing less than the repudiation of enforced ortho-doxy in church and state. Anchoring duty in the word of God as understood by the autonomous individual who is guided by reason alone fractured the link which the Reformation Church of England had worked long and hard to establish between the need for institu-tional guidance and everyone's main goal in life: personal salvation. The *Essay* shattered the intellectual underpinnings of the confessional state, just as the Toleration Act of 1689 ended the Church of England's monopoly over theological and moral discipline. Doctrine and instruc-tion, knowledge and belief; all had been reduced to the sanctity of the individual soul. Whatever influence the Church of England continued to wield in the political sphere throughout the course of the eighteenth century due to the not unimportant fact that Dissenters were not accorded political rights by the Toleration Act of 1689, the disen-chantment with the authority of the priest had been accorded powerful philosophic credentials with the *Essay*, a work at once anticlerical and deeply religious. It was a revolutionary, but at the same time a remarkably restorative intellectual accomplishment.

3

THE HETERODOXY OF A SIMPLE FAITH

In a postscript to his first reply to Bishop of Worcester Edward Stillingfleet in 1697, Locke stated unequivocally that 'The holy scripture is to me, and always will be, the constant guide of my assent; and I shall always hearken to it, as containing infallible truth, relating to things of the highest concernment.' Read today, these words appear strangely disconsonant with the historical image of Locke as a proponent of minimalist, anti-trinitarian, and rational Christianity, of a faith without enigma and lacking the transcendent appeal of the numinous. Indeed, in the very same postscript to Stillingfleet, Locke proceeded to confess that while there were many mysteries in the Bible, he had no reservations about accepting these as true accounts 'because God has said it: and I shall presently condemn and quit any opinion of mine, as soon as I am shown that it is contrary to any revelation in the holy scripture'. In a subsequent reply to Stillingfleet's attack on the epistemology of the *Essay*, Locke insisted that he had always 'read the revelation of the holy scripture with a full assurance that all it delivers is true'.[1]

Here were sentiments not so entirely dissimilar from those of the former Augustinian monk Martin Luther, sentiments very much at the core of a system of reformed belief which instinctively accepted the veracity of the word of God unencumbered by the expanding boundaries of natural theology. One of those who delivered the unmediated word of God, St Paul, was for Locke divinely inspired because he 'made noe use of any humane science improvement or skil; no insinuations of Eloquence; no philosophical speculations, or ornaments of humane learning'.[2] For a man who had purportedly undermined

53

the very foundations of the Christian order with his novel way of ideas in the *Essay*, Locke could sound at times very much like those early Protestant reformers who wished to place their entire trust in the unmediated and inerrant word of God. George Santayana seemed to recognize as much when he observed some 60 years ago that one of the most important presuppositions in Locke's mind was his 'confident and sincere' Christian faith.[3] Indeed his call in the *Essay* for his contemporaries 'to spend the days of this our Pilgrimage with Industry and Care, in the search, and following of that way, which might lead us to a State of greater Perfection,' echoed the pleadings of saints and mystics from the earliest age of the faith.[4]

Like so many others of his generation who had both observed and experienced first-hand the English wars of truth, Locke was deeply interested in religion even as a young man at Oxford when he was afforded opportunities to study medicine and natural philosophy. It cannot be stressed enough that Locke considered it to be a fundamental Christian duty that each person read and study the Bible. It was, in addition to a moral life, part of one's work of obedience to God. His was an attention to Scripture which deepened as he grew older, and it is attested by the many references to theological treatises, biblical commentaries, and to the Old and New Testaments in his unpublished journals. Familiarity with theological subjects was, of course, not uncommon for educated men in the seventeenth century, particularly in light of the standard university curriculum. But the intensity of Locke's application to the subject is considerable, and is clearly evidenced in each of his major works; in fact most of what he wrote, regardless of the immediate topic, was informed by an underlying religious agenda. His contemporaries seemed to recognize this deliberate, God-centred agenda better, certainly, than did his eighteenth-century popularizers. The controversies in which Locke reluctantly found himself engaged during the last 14 years of his life involved the very sort of ill-tempered wrangling over religious matters that were so distasteful to him, and in his estimation it was these incessant quarrels that were contributing factors to Europe's on-going intolerance and state-supported violence. He was not called upon to defend the political ideas expressed in *Two Treatises* after its publication in 1690, nor did educators take exception to his recommendations for tutoring the child published in *Some Thoughts Concerning Education*. It was on religious and moral grounds alone that Locke's work was scrutinized and attacked, by churchmen and non-jurors alike, for introducing ideas likely to shatter the very cornerstone principles of the historic faith.

A catalogue of his final library reflects Locke's deep engagement with religion. Of the books owned by Locke, 28 per cent or 870 titles, belong, broadly speaking, to the category of theology.[5] All of his major published works contain extended discussions of religious matters, and his posthumously published *A Paraphrase and Notes on the Epistles of St. Paul* (1705) attests to the depth and lucidity of his study and exposition. He owned 28 Bibles printed in the sixteenth and seventeenth centuries, including editions in Latin, Greek, Hebrew, English, and one in Dutch. In addition, two dozen copies of the New Testament, representing Greek, Latin, French, Italian, Spanish and Syriac languages, are included in the final catalogue. In both *Some Thoughts Concerning Education* and 'Directions for Reading and Study for a Gentleman' written the year before his death, Locke recommended Scripture, and especially the New Testament, as the single best source for the principles of morality and ethics. In light of the diversity of his lifetime literary output, we can perhaps be grateful that Locke declined to take holy orders while holding his Studentship at Christ Church, but one should not interpret his wish to remain outside the official life of the Church as a disinclination to engage in and attempt to resolve pressing theological questions.

Acute religious turmoil marked the entire span of Locke's century, first in the struggle between Puritan and Anglican visions of the true church during his boyhood years of the 1630s and 1640s, later after the Restoration in the efforts of the re-established Church to extinguish nonconformity by means of intimidation and criminal sanction, and finally after the accession of William and Mary with the emergence of the Deist or rationalist threat to traditional Revelation. And although we know frustratingly little about Locke's church-going, his interest in religious matters was always pursued from within the ambit of the Church of England, to which he repeatedly declared his allegiance in his writings.[6]

His friends within the Church after the mid-1660s, the latitudinarian divines, appealed to Locke's growing sense of the need for a faith which, in the words of Galatians 5:6, 'worketh by love'. He was already familiar with the work of earlier Arminians such as Henry Hammond, John Hales, and Richard Allestree when he moved to London in 1667, and he had probably come to reject the Calvinist notion of justification by faith alone – a position advocated by John

Owen at Christ Church while Locke was still an undergraduate – before he moved into Shaftesbury's home. Latitudinarians such as John Tillotson, Simon Patrick, and Edward Fowler, in their common-sense exigetical style, questioned the validity of righteousness by faith alone, and instead stressed that a working faith was preliminary to justification. They also believed that Revelation was largely a restatement of natural law, and that natural law was accessible to human reason. The advantage of access to Revelation was that God's word both clarified the precepts of natural law and provided powerful incentives for obedience. The latitudinarians did not hesitate to link obedience with both temporal and eternal happiness; they believed that virtue in this life led to unrivalled rewards in heaven. They also affirmed that self-interest and morality were intimately connected, while the indwelling of the spirit of God was reduced in importance as the sole inspiration to the practice of good works.[7]

Locke shared each of these positions with the latitudinarians by the late 1660s. He also endorsed their conviction that the essentials of the faith were few and simple, that human fallibility was the strongest evidence against imposing one's religious views on another, that heresy must be linked with the will and not with a mere failure of understanding, and, finally, that while some religious truths may be above the grasp of reason, none was contradictory to reason.[8] The believer was always to govern his assent to religious propositions on the basis of the evidence, and never on the mere word of authority. Nonconformists who made claims to religious truth which avoided the test of reasonable evidence in favour of the inward working of grace were relegated to the category of 'enthusiasts', those who would arrogantly avoid the hard work of critical evaluation and freely impose their views on others.

Each of these latitudinarian positions would find a place in Locke's later *Reasonableness of Christianity* and in *A Paraphrase and Notes Upon the Epistles of St. Paul*. Locke did not accept the latitudinarian perspective in its entirety, however. None of his clergy friends would join him in his 1667 call for toleration, nor, for obvious reasons, did they share his desire for a diminution of clerical influence in affairs of state, his rejection of the principle of natural superiors. By the 1680s Locke had established additional friendships with men who embraced a wide variety of heterodox opinions, some of whom were Socinians or Deists. Socinians were faulted and condemned for denying a wide sweep of orthodox positions: the pre-existence of Christ before the Virgin birth, the atoning work of the Saviour, the doctrine of the Trinity, the incapacitating stain of original sin, and eternal punishment for the wicked. Deists were also accused of anti-trinitarianism, but their main fault seems to have been their vocal distrust of Revelation. At the time when Locke's publishing career got underway in 1689, several unorthodox movements had their representatives in print, and in such a climate all innovations were viewed by the defenders of tradition as overt, or, what was even more pernicious, covert threats to the established Church.[9] The fact that Locke had forged a number of close friendships during his six-year exile in Holland (1683–9) with men whose religious views were decidedly unorthodox made his later connection with the English Deist Anthony Collins and with the London Socinian Thomas Firmin appear all the more suspect.

In reality, as with his latitudinarian associations, Locke found much to admire in anyone who appreciated the importance of reason to religion and the need for a critical approach to Scripture, and these qualities were certainly exhibited by the heterodox with whom he now affiliated. In an age of increasingly bold and trenchant challenges to the ancient Christian story, many forwarded by the men whom he knew and respected, Locke continued to adhere to the central principle of early Reformation theology: individual access to, interpretation of, and unflinching trust in God's dictate for humankind. Like those first reformers, Locke accepted that the Bible was an accurate record of events whose truth was authenticated by miracles. Whatever perceived threats to orthodoxy his work may have involved, whatever wanderings from official church teaching his speculations may have entailed, whatever anticlericalism it promoted, Locke's design at every juncture was to refer his critics back to the life-saving text, in effect obliging his detractors to identify precisely where his allegedly novel conclusions overstepped the plain message contained in Scripture.

Late in life, in his 'Second Vindication of the *Reasonableness of Christianity*', Locke sardonically observed that: 'If the reading and study of the Scripture were more pressed than it is, and men were fairly sent to the Bible to find their religion; and not the Bible put into their hands only to find the opinions of their particular sect or party: Christendom would have more Christians, and those that are would be more knowing and more in the right than they now are.'[10] Convinced by the late 1660s that the arbitrary imposition of official doctrine by clerical elites undermined the core of the original Reformation spirit and made men lazy adherents of doctrines which they did not understand, Locke stressed a theology of simple precepts, guideposts and injunctions that any reasonable student of the Word could elicit for himself through a private and reflective examination of Holy Writ. In a Europe where the use of force to achieve religious conformity had failed to establish that the persecuting party was closer to the truth than the persecuted, the achievement of outward obedience and uniformity of doctrine was for Locke a hollow and irrelevant victory.

The seventeenth and eighteenth centuries in England, John Yolton has recently reminded us, were marked 'by a general and persistent concern about threats to orthodoxy in religion', and in particular by a fear of a drift towards Deism and atheism.[11] And during the Restoration, Church of England orthodoxy included acceptance of a fairly long list of tenets to be taken on faith: the legitimacy of Revelation and miracle; the Mosaic story of creation and our sin-stained descent from Adam; the doctrine of the Trinity; the reality of incorporeal or spiritual substance; the eternity of reward or punishment after judgement; the goal of a Christian commonwealth superintended by the state church. These repesented but a few of the chief marks of Anglican belief, and anyone who questioned the consensus was promptly labelled heterodox or, what was worse, atheist, by skilful – and oftentimes quarrelsome – defenders of the status quo.

Despite his early writings on church–state relations, his biblical criticisms of Sir Robert Filmer's *Patriarcha*, and his connections with the latitudinarian divines of the city of London, Locke did not appear to concern himself in any sustained manner with theological questions until the time of his exile to Holland in 1683. But when he did begin to address these centuries-old concerns, he found that his interpretation of Scripture placed him in disagreement with a good part of the established canon of the Church with which he had always identified himself. For example, his understanding of the future life after death broke with the widely accepted and officially endorsed notion of bodily resurrection followed by eternal life with God or eternal torment with Satan. We also find that Locke put forward a definition of the soul in his *Essay* which was sharply at odds with the traditional picture of the thinking, immaterial substance. Nowhere in his work do we find him criticizing the doctrine of the Trinity, but neither (after 1662) does he affirm this core tenet of the Church, even when pressed to do so by respected opponents like Stillingfleet. Finally, his analysis of original sin and its impact on Adam's descendants appeared to overturn the age-old picture of men and women who were burdened with guilt for the first transgression, a guilt which thoroughly incapacitated them for works pleasing to God. A brief examination of each of these problems will illustrate Locke's theological independence, his refusal to accept guidance beyond his own discernment of the text. It will also serve to show how Locke's 'priesthood of all believers', exercising mature reason and committed to a plain reading of the text, could place him beyond the bounds of established orthodoxy in the late seventeenth century.

Perhaps the most fundamental challenge facing any organized religion throughout the ages involves how it interprets the mystery of the individual's prospects after death. In seventeenth-century England the reality of an early or a sudden death from a host of sources which no longer trouble inhabitants of the modern West certainly provided ample occasion for the faithful to reflect upon the rich contours of the Christian explanation of life beyond the veil.[12] Broadly speaking, the Christian view of reality has always been a plural one. In other words, it was the accepted wisdom of the Roman Catholic Church that discrete persons or individual souls continue to persist after organic death in another, eternal realm separate from the body. Both elements would then be reunited at the final judgement or 'Great Assize'. By and large, Protestant reformers accepted the established Catholic definition. They agreed that the 'person' was composed of two distinct substances, one material and the other immaterial, and that the second of these, while unfortunately beyond the ken of sense experience, operated the body and constituted the strongest grounds for a belief in human immortality. Ever since the early Church Fathers had abandoned the Hebrew unitive or monistic understanding of man as an animated body and developed in its place the notion, built upon Greek foundations, of an incarnate soul which bears the image of its divine Maker, commentators had maintained that there was a basic difference between the temporary body and the incorruptible soul, with the soul constituting the central element. At the moment of death, it was believed, the flesh returns to dust to await the resurrection, while the immaterial soul substance immediately experiences a foretaste of divine reward or retribution. The pleasure, or alternatively, the suffering, is sharply intensified, beginning at the last day and continuing throughout eternity when the same material body is reunited with the indestructible spiritual substance.[13]

Post-mortem expiation or atonement was of course excluded with the abolition of the Roman Catholic purgatory, but there remained nevertheless a qualitative difference between the experience of the soul after death and the fate of both body and soul reunited after judge-

ment. As one of Locke's latitudinarian friends, Gilbert Burnet, indicated in his influential *Exposition of the Thirty-Nine Articles of the Church
of England* (1699), since St Paul had represented judgement day as the
moment when full blessedness was bestowed upon the deserving, it
should surprise no one 'that from hence some have thought upon very
probable grounds, that the blessed, though admitted to happiness
immediately upon their death, yet were not so completely happy as
they shall be at the Resurrection'. On the other hand, the same sense
of progression from death to judgement affected the sinful soul as well.
In his *Whole Parable of Dives and Lazarus* (1697), for example, Joseph
Stevens stated that the soul in hell before judgement has little to do
except to look forward to the terrible day with dread and fear 'wherin
it must change its unhappy condition for a much worse'.[14]

This powerful analysis of the relationship between body and soul,
centuries in the making and widely thought to provide the most
satisfactory argument for the uniqueness of humanity in the variety
of creation, was communicated widely in the pulpit, in learned
treatises, and in formal debate throughout the course of the seventeenth century.[15] Yet in spite of the strong official sanction given to this
dualistic view of the afterlife over the centuries, there had always been
a latent danger that one or the other of the component parts, the first
characterized by extension and the second by thought, would be
subtracted from the essential core at the moment of death. The notion
of a disembodied spirit as somehow necessary to life after death was,
after all, a rather late development in Hebrew thought, and dualism
had encountered a number of so-called 'mortalist' critics throughout
the course of Western church history, men who demurred at the
prospect of an active soul after death but before final judgement.
Aside from the more obvious inconsistency involved in a view which
held that both body and soul were essential to personhood but which
simultaneously maintained that body could be temporarily discharged
between death and resurrection, these mortalist opponents were quick
to point out that there was no explicit mention made in the New
Testament of an immortal soul similar in any substantive respect to
that being advanced by theologians, that in fact the word 'immortal'
occurs only three times, and then in connection with the risen Christ.[16]

The orthodox response to these mortalist challenges had always
been to stress that while the soul is indeed separated from the body at
death, neither body nor soul alone constitutes a complete human
being. The second-century Bishop Irenaeus, for example, had maintained that 'Spirit with the flesh taken away would not be a spiritual

man, but the spirit of a man' while much later Aquinas pointedly observed that 'My soul is not I, and if only souls are saved, I am not saved, nor is any man'.[17] Such views were predicated upon the physicalist understanding of Jesus's resurrection which had been advanced in all four gospels and in the Acts of the Apostles. The soul's journey between death and resurrection constituted an attenuated and incomplete form of existence. Only when God miraculously raises our bodies at the judgement can it be said that we are whole persons again.

As the body gradually became the centrepiece of the Christian memorial event, witnessed not least by the elaborate funeral preparations undertaken to preserve the corpse throughout the late medieval and early modern periods, so too the case for the centrality of the organism, mere matter, advanced in discussions of post-mortem affairs.[18] This elevation of the importance of the body in Christian thought provided the starting point for Locke's investigation of the relationship between matter or organism and what he defined as the 'person' who will be judged at the close of history. And it was his novel diminution of the importance of the body, or at least the same body over time, which occasioned one of his more significant breaks with orthodoxy.

Locke's treatment of the post-mortem question is to be found scattered throughout his published and unpublished remains, and most directly in his protracted exchange with Edward Stillingfleet between 1697 and 1698. Locke affirmed in *The Reasonableness of Christianity* that there would be a general resurrection, made possible by the death and return to life of the Messiah, and Stillingfleet did not question the sincerity of these statements.[19] In fact resurrection and judgement were essential to Locke's view of moral obligations in a world where God would punish and reward according to the individual's merits. But Stillingfleet did maintain that Locke's 'way of ideas' and his definition of person in the *Essay* were inconsistent with the traditional understanding of restoration to life at the day of judgement. Stillingfleet, like so many other churchmen, had taken no objection to Locke's *Essay* before 1696. But the publication of *The Reasonableness of Christianity* in 1695, followed by the appearance (anonymously) of John Toland's *Christianity Not Mysterious* in 1696, led the bishop to revisit the potential implications of Locke's philosophy for the Christian faith. In *A Discourse in Vindication of the Doctrine of the Trinity* (1697) Stillingfleet coupled Locke's *Essay* with Toland's book, referring to both authors as 'the new men of ideas'.

The conventional Anglican view of the resurrection – and the one endorsed by Stillingfleet – stressed that an identical material body would be restored to life at the moment of Christ's return, recoupled with the soul, and adjudicated in terms of actions carried out during the person's lifetime. The problem concerning the age of the resurrected body had been resolved, to the satisfaction of most observers at least, by theologians who had taken Christ's age at the time of his death as the optimum point of restoration. This compromise had its obvious difficulties, not the least of which was a seventeenth-century mortality rate which claimed the lives of one quarter of the population before they reached their fifteenth birthday. Still it was thought to be important that a mature person who understood the consequences of his actions be placed in the docket for the lofty proceedings, and the power of God was normally invoked in order to address the many exceptions to the agreed formula.

In the first three editions of the *Essay* Locke had spoken of the resurrection 'of our Bodies' on the assumption, as he later told Stillingfleet, that Scripture taught the return of the earthly vessel.[20] Indeed up until the 1690s he most likely believed in the orthodox return of the same body at the end of historic time, even though in his essay 'Of Study' from 1677 he had placed the question of what type of body we will have at the resurrection into the camp of 'remote useless speculations'.[21] But in the fourth edition (1700) this passage was altered to read 'the Dead' reflecting the author's return to Scripture in the wake of his letters from Stillingfleet. He had assumed, erroneously, that Scripture had mentioned the resurrection of the same body. In the course of his dialogue with Stillingfleet, Locke pointed out the absurdity of supposing that the same identical organism continues to exist throughout a person's lifetime. He told his opponent 'that the body he had, when an embryo in the womb, when a child playing in coats, when a man marrying a wife, and when bed-rid, dying of a consumption, and at last, which he shall have after his resurrection' are each owned by the person as their unique body, but cannot constitute the same identical body.[22] When Locke later had an opportunity to apply his hermeneutical method to the epistles to the Corinthians, he firmly endorsed St Paul's description of spiritualized bodies at the resurrection, minus the elements of earthly matter and free from the limitations imposed on the ever-changing material component. For his part Stillingfleet acknowledged that particles of matter in the body are lost and change throughout the course of one's period on earth, but he continued to insist that an essential material substance, united to an immaterial and ethereal soul and constant from birth to death to resurrection, was key to explaining personal identity over time.

Stillingfleet's death in 1699 ended the voluminous exchange between the two men, but Locke continued to reflect on the matter of the future state. Beginning *A Paraphrase and Notes on the Epistles of St. Paul* after the bishop's death, Locke reaffirmed his amended position, insisting that the apostle Paul wrote that God 'can give to men at the resurrection bodys of very different constitutions and qualitys from those they had before'.[23] Flesh and blood cannot enter into the kingdom, and if St Paul is to be trusted, 'Nor are such fleeting corruptible things as our present bodys' capable of entry 'to that state of immutable incorruptibility'.[24] Adherence to Scripture also accounts for his later silence on the question of the interregnum between death and resurrection. In the 1660s he had written of the 'strong probability amounting allmost to certainty that he [God] will put the soules of men into a state of life or perception after the dissolution of those bodys', but in the 1690s this confidence was no longer expressed.[25] Some of the ancients had offered 'obscure' and 'uncertain' arguments in favour of some form of conscious existence after death, but for the most part these pictures of the afterlife were the inventions of wit and ornaments of poetry, each of which, in Locke's estimation, rendered them suspect.[26] Locke's conviction that immortality was awarded after the resurrection made it appear that he had entered a mortalist camp now distinguished by the names of Thomas Hobbes and John Milton, but for his own part he did not wish to comment where the text did not provide guidance.

In the final analysis, Locke did not think that the traditional doctrine of immaterial substance or soul was essential to resurrection, particularly since in the *Essay* he had argued that we can have no clear idea of substance as a metaphysical concept in the first place. Our ideas originated from sensation and reflection alone, and the senses could not afford us access to the real essences of things, a position once again challenged by Stillingfleet. Rather it was the person, defined by Locke as sameness of consciousness and acceptance of responsibility for actions undertaken in this life, which would be judged on the final day. Unlike man, the biological organism who shares a host of traits with plants and animals, person, as we saw in chapter 2, was a forensic term appropriating action and its merit. Personhood is something each one of us acquires over the course of our education into rationality from childhood, and God is interested solely in the moral component at judgement, not in the biological unit which provides but a temporary vehicle for the person. In a manner that troubled his harshest critics, Locke wished to locate personal identity in consciousness rather than in a substance about which we could only know qualities and attributes. For his own part, the emphasis on person instead of body and soul strengthened the commitment to a morally based, action-oriented Christian theology.

According to the established metaphysics of Locke's day, the essence of any person or thing was believed to be some property without which the existence of the person or thing would not be possible. For immaterial substance or soul, that essential property was the power of uninterrupted thought, and it was widely agreed that only immaterial substance enjoyed this power. But at the opening of Book 2 of the *Essay*, Locke asserted that while thought was indeed one attribute or product of immaterial substance, it was by no means an inseparable or defining characteristic.[27] This bold declaration was openly at odds with the Cartesian and traditional Christian account, but for Locke the force of commonsense experience told us that thought does not even commence prior to the acquisition of ideas built upon sense after birth, while we have no solid evidence of thought taking place when we are asleep. How could one ascribe deliberate mental activity to someone who had no recollection of thinking while asleep or unconscious?[28] In addition to this controversial statement, Locke observed in a casual comment that an omnipotent God might even superadd the power of thought to matter if He were so inclined, a position which drew an immediate rebuttal from Stillingfleet.[29] Richard Bentley joined in the attack on Locke in his Second Boyle Lecture (1694), maintaining that matter was incapable of accommodating thought, not because of any shortcoming on God's part, but due rather to 'an incapacity in the subject'.[30] For latitudinarians such as Locke, on the other hand, experience suggested that God exercised His power according to the principles of reason; but human reason was not to be the sole standard by which God was to be confined. As Locke told Stillingfleet, he had nowhere in the *Essay* stated that God *had* given the power of thought to matter, nor had he endorsed the dangerous idea that matter, without God's special intervention, could think, but that he saw no contradiction in the prospect of thinking matter if one took into account the distance between the ambit of human reason and its divine counterpart. In an uncharacteristic digression from Scripture, Locke reminded Stillingfleet that even the Fathers of the early Church refused to deny God the power to add sensation, perception, and thought to matter.[31]

While never directly questioning the sincerity of Locke's claim that he believed in the resurrection of the dead, Stillingfleet held that both of these novel positions advanced the cause of materialist interpretations of reality and gave comfort to atheists who would gladly do away with the whole idea of immaterial substance. If, as Locke was suggesting, the soul was no longer to be defined as a thinking substance, if thought were a bare contingency or accident originating in sense data, and if simple extended matter might think, then what would be the need for maintaining an ontological dualism which involved the always difficult task of explaining the nature of the interaction between matter and spirit? Whether or not Locke agreed with them, opponents of the faith could now claim philosophical underpinnings for their heresy. The spectre of atheism built upon the foundations of materialism burdened orthodox churchmen throughout the final half of the century, even though openly atheistic works were not to be found in print.[32] Even Locke acknowledged that atheism dissolved the bonds of society because those who denied God were incapable of living up to oaths and solemn agreements, and he called for atheists to be 'shut out of all sober and civil society'.[33] But for those alarmed by Locke's position on God's power, the possibility of thinking matter led first to the removal of spirit as a separate substance and ultimately to the dissolution of God-ordained human order.

In any treatment of life after death during Locke's day, the question of punishment for those who rejected the divine precepts contained in Scripture was never ignored. Throughout the medieval and early modern periods, the doctrine of hell and unending perdition for the unrepentant sinner had been both a centrepiece of Christian eschatology and an essential bulwark of social discipline and the status quo. Anchored in the authority of Scripture (especially Matt. 25:46, Rev. 14:10–11 and Rev. 20:10) and seconded by a wide variety of patristic sources, there had been few dissenters from the official teaching until well after the Reformation had fractured the religious unity of Western Europe. According to the orthodox reading, once body and soul were reunited at judgement, the entire person, if self-condemned by his earthly actions, would be cast aside into a world of torment without end. The lonely judgement of the individual at the moment of death was now completed by the very public tribunal at the close of historic time, and each sinner would be condemned to unspeakable suffering before an unprecedented gathering of all humanity. Every rhetorical device available was employed in the pulpit to describe the misery of the damned in hell, both as a means of regulating behaviour in a society where the coercive apparatus of the state was limited and in an attempt to improve the eternal prospects of those still living.

Recent scholarly treatments of hell have pointed to an abatement – and in some cases even an abandonment – of belief in unending torment, beginning at the close of the seventeenth century. This depreciation of hell was produced, it is argued, by a combination of improving material conditions by 1700 and a shift in emphasis respecting God's principal characteristics. A benevolent deity, it was now assumed, would never subject humanity to unending affliction for finite sins committed in a fleeting and fragile state. Locke certainly endorsed the notion of a compassionate deity who desired the salvation of the largest number, but his novel analysis of Adam's fate, and the fate of Adam's progeny before Christ assumed a human form on earth, encouraged contemporary advocates of soul-sleeping such as Henry Layton and William Coward, together with later historians who have examined *The Reasonableness of Christianity* with this issue in mind, to suggest that Locke may have accepted the annihilation or death of the body *and soul* at the moment of judgement.[34]

This reading of Locke's intentions is based largely upon statements made by the author in the opening pages of *The Reasonableness*. There, in the course of re-examining what it was that Adam had lost in paradise, Locke observed that the death imposed on the first man and woman and their posterity meant 'nothing but a ceasing to be, the losing of all actions of life and sense'.[35] Had the first man not violated God's single injunction in that state, he and his posterity would have lived forever. Following his own hermeneutic injunction to read the text for its unadorned meaning, Locke argued that it would be unreasonable to place any other signification on the word death in Scripture, and he compared any effort to associate simple expiration of body with eternal punishment to the fantastic prospect of keeping a felon who is sentenced to death for his crimes in eternal torment here on earth. Taken together with Locke's silence (in this work and elsewhere) regarding the status of the person between death and resurrection, and his assertion in the *Essay* that the immateriality of the soul was not necessary to resurrection, mortalists were quick to claim his endorsement of their radical alternative to traditional eschatology.

The claims of the mortalists were not without merit, for *The Reasonableness* does not establish a consistent posture on the fate of the damned. Locke initially indicated that 'an exclusion from paradise and loss of immortality is the portion of sinners', but later spoke of eternal misery, 'pain of hell-fire', 'unspeakable rewards and punishments' being the final lot of the wicked. He also quoted St Matthew's reference to a furnace of fire where there shall be wailing and gnashing of teeth in what can only be interpreted as a familiar effort to describe the torments of hell and insisted, on the basis of the text in Matthew, that the fire would be everlasting for the unrepentant sinner. The earlier *Essay* contained similar ambiguity. In Book 2 the author spoke of 'Rewards and Punishments, of infinite weight and duration, in another Life' but again suggested that a 'dreadful state of Misery' may overtake the guilty, 'or at best the terrible uncertain hope of Annihilation'.[36] The non-juror John Milner noticed Locke's inconsistent statements in *The Reasonableness* over the eternal fate of persons and brought it to public attention in 1700, but Locke did not reply to his criticism.[37]

In an unpublished paper probably written in 1699, however, after he had engaged Bishop Stillingfleet on the nature of the resurrection, Locke appeared to endorse the annihilationist position – at least as far as the destiny of the sinner was concerned. Portions of this paper were ultimately incorporated into Locke's long note on 1 Corinthians XV.42 in the *Paraphrase* and first published in 1706. In this paper, and in the published note, Locke proposed that Paul was only referring to the just, and not the wicked, when discussing the nature of the resurrection, even though the apostle used 'the general name of the resurrection of the dead' in the epistle.[38] The fate of the undeserving is not described by St Paul, other than to infer that they are not worthy of eternal life. In the 1699 paper Locke pointed to passages in Luke, John, and in Paul's Epistle to the Romans where the unjust are condemned to death and not eternal hellfire, and he cited a controversial sermon by his deceased friend Archbishop Tillotson as further evidence that the prospect of annihilation for the wicked after judgement is indeed scriptural. The reference was both unfortunate and misleading, for Tillotson, who had died in 1694, had merely used the occasion in his sermon to suggest the possibility of God remitting a sentence as another example of divine power and not to affirm the truth of annihilation.

For Locke a new covenant had been introduced by Christ on the Cross, and with it came the assurance of continued, indeed eternal life beyond the grave for the saint, while the status of the damned broke with the orthodox view of unending torment. This immortality for saints was not the inherent right or essence of the human spirit; it was rather a gift bestowed on the faithful, while extinction was the punishment ultimately inflicted upon the sinner. In the *Essays on the Law of Nature* he had established this by remarking that 'God has created us out of nothing and, if He pleases, will reduce us again to nothing'.[39] Immortality for the obedient was a morally significant continuation made possible by extraordinary means; extinction had its moral gravity as well, but as it was without pain and suffering, Locke's critics understandably equated it with an endorsement of unrestrained behaviour in this life. At the very least it approached the Socinian position on the matter and presented a dilemma for his moral theory where reward and punishment were the key motives to Christian, life-saving conduct.[40]

Locke's exclusion of thought as the defining characteristic of immaterial substance in the *Essay*, together with his silence regarding the state of the soul between death and resurrection, had the appearance of lending credibility to the soul-sleeping and annihilationist hypotheses outlined in the posthumously published notes on St Paul's epistles. For if one accepted, as Locke did in the *Essay*, that the soul substance was not always thinking during our earthly probation, then the possibility of the total cessation of thought after death became more plausible. And by following his exegetical mandate not to speculate where Scripture was silent, Locke refused to be drawn into the quagmire over the state of the soul between death and resurrection. As even a cursory look at seventeenth-century efforts to distinguish between the status of the soul after death but before judgement will reveal, English Protestants had generally failed in their efforts to find an emotionally and intellectually satisfying alternative to the Catholic purgatory. Speculation about the nature of the afterlife for soul and body was normally avoided by the latitudinarian divines, men whose main interest was in shaping conduct along the lines prescribed by Scripture. This natural reticence was coupled with an epistemology that cautioned against the erection of formal doctrine where scriptural foundation was lacking. When John Tillotson confessed that we did not possess the highest level of evidence for a future life, which to him was the evidence of sense and personal experience, but that we did possess a second level of evidence, what he called the evidence provided by 'persons every way credible' he was speaking the language of the *Essay* and *The Reasonableness of Christianity*. The testimony of God through his Son and the general consent of mankind were for Tillotson, and for Locke, sufficient evidence of the veracity of their respective pictures of the afterlife where rewards and punishments would be apportioned.[41]

Both Locke's concept of person and his approach to reading Scripture made the historic doctrine of the Trinity, one of the benchmarks of existing orthodoxy, difficult to support. Since the early centuries of the Church, the idea of God as Father, Son and Holy Spirit – three persons but one substance – had been one of the central mysteries of the Christian faith which distinguished it from Judaism and Islam. Originating in a felt need to settle difficulties regarding the relationship between a Christ who prayed to the Father yet with whom he claimed to be one (i.e. John 10:30), the terminology of one being in three persons and the term 'Trinity' goes back at least to Tertullian at the start of the third century. Later, at the fourth-century councils at Nicea (325) and at Constantinople (381) the doctrine was advanced as a weapon in the struggle against the Arian heresy. In addition to Christ's relationship to the Father, the Holy Spirit is repeatedly mentioned in New Testament writings, and some need to accommodate this term into the Godhead was thought to be necessary. Since the time of St Augustine the notion of three distinctions within one divine reality had been accepted by the Catholic Church as best fitted to describe the threefold activity of God: creation, redemption, and sanctification. God the Father was temporally immune, God the Son temporally involved in mission and passion, and God the Spirit communicated the gifts of the timeless to mankind in an earthly setting.

While pressed on the issue by Stillingfleet, Locke refused to oblige the bishop by declaring his acceptance of the Trinity, claiming repeatedly that his *Essay* was not written with the purpose of arbitrating the on-going dispute between anti-trinitarians and their orthodox opponents. That dispute, unfortunately for Locke, had reached its height by the 1690s, and when Parliament responded in 1696 with an Act for repressing atheism by making it a crime to deny 'any one of the persons of the holy Trinity to be God', Locke's predicament intensified. Apart from the fact that Locke was naturally eager to stay clear of any possible legal entanglements, as a Christian philosopher attempting to persuade a Christian audience, he was careful not to condemn doctrines which he may not have shared with the majority. His technical definition of the person as a morally responsible individual clearly did not ally comfortably with the metaphysical mystery of three persons in one substance, although he did not, understandably, attempt to highlight this awkward point. But the fact that he did not include the doctrine of the Trinity in his list of beliefs necessary

before one could be called a Christian placed him under strong
suspicion of Unitarian sympathies. More significantly, and perhaps
in the end more provocatively, he told Stillingfleet that his Bible said
nothing about 'three persons in one nature, or there are two natures
and one person'.[42] And when the clergyman John Edwards published
a vituperative attack on *The Reasonableness* in 1695, Locke quickly
responded with the same emphatic recourse to Scripture, accusing
Edwards of mistaking atheism for any notions in disagreement with his
own fixed prejudices.[43] John Marshall has argued convincingly that
Locke was most likely a Unitarian by the mid 1690s at the latest, and
the fact that his Bible-based faith did not mention the doctrine of the
Trinity adds additional plausibility to this conclusion.

Locke tells us that the principal occasion for *The Reasonableness of
Christianity* was his own dissatisfaction with existing systems of theology
and doctrine, all of which began by harnessing the text to existing
philosophical systems, and none of which seemed to encourage the
spirit of rational inquiry into Scripture which he believed lay at the
heart of the Reformation. In particular, this anonymously published
little book sought to explore the entire sweep of that which was
required to be believed before one could legitimately be called a
Christian. The answer was, for critics like John Edwards, alarming
in its brevity, although Locke claimed that his conclusions were based
entirely upon a reading of the text which was guided by the original
intentions of the unlettered but inspired authors. One had to freely
accept Christ as Messiah before entering into the family of believing
Christians, Locke insisted, and beyond this one austere tenet, there was
no need to pursue, much less to enjoin, additional doctrine. Of course
Locke maintained that belief in Christ as Messiah automatically
entailed belief that the Son of God had died and been resurrected as
a propitiation for the sins of humankind, and that he would return to
judgement at the close of history, but even with this significant
addition the traditional doctrinal programme had been drastically
attenuated, presaging serious consequences for a sacrametally based
and hierarchically organized established Church. Locke also observed
that the true Christian would evidence his faith by living in accordance with a morality based upon the New Testament, thereby
confirming his impatience with the notion that adherence to the
theologians' creeds and the establishment's rituals was an adequate
measure of one's faith.

The Reasonableness was clearly informed by the memory of conflicting
claims to religious authority witnessed during the years of civil war, by

the bitter antagonism highlighting the relationship between orthodoxy and dissent after 1660, and by the flurry of renewed debate after the accession of William and Mary in 1689. No doubt Locke's intense disdain for religious enthusiasm, so forcefully presented in chapter 22 of the fourth edition of the *Essay*, also contributed to the composition of his survey. But *The Reasonabless of Christianity* is, in addition, a work concerned with the consequences of the historic fall of Adam, and of the many results outlined by Locke the most important was the apparent inability of man to obey God's law in full and thus merit salvation as a debt discharged. Since the original covenant of works required unimpaired obedience to the divine mandate, a gracious Saviour now offered a new covenant, one where faith takes the place of full righteousness. And the object of that faith, according to Locke, is not to be understood by reason alone; Messiahship and all that it entails transcends mere ratiocination. It is useful to recall that for Locke his conclusions were always the product of personal and sustained exegesis, certainly the prerogative of no one person, but a critical method which he believed, much like the earliest sixteenth-century Protestant reformers, would lead to consensus regarding fundamentals if the inquirer employed reason as his steady guide in the review of Scripture. If, as he believed, those fundamentals were seen in all their simplicity and rigour, perhaps then holy living would take the place of fractious theology as the pre-eminent concern of those in the pulpit.

Locke mentions Revelation, or God's extraordinary communication to his creatures, quite frequently in his published writings, and its importance was dramatically enhanced as he failed to carry out the proposal, introduced in the *Essay* and subsequently encouraged by his friend William Molyneux, whereby universal moral rules might be discovered and followed by reason alone.[44] As we saw in chapter 2, by 1695 Locke had acknowledged that reason had never made out the contents of the law of nature in its entirety. In fact as the *Essay* outlined the limits of our knowledge, while offering no progress toward a demonstrative morality, it became imperative for Locke to provide some alternative ground on which men might shape their actions.[45] He had specifically defined Revelation in the *Essay* as 'Natural reason enlarged by a new set of Discoveries communicated by God immediately, which Reason vouches the Truth of, by the Testimony and Proofs it gives, that they come from God' and he described faith as our assent to Revelation.[46] Such a definition was intended to preclude the advance of reckless and harmful enthusiasm, but it also left room for truths which were unavailable to reason, truths which included the resurrection from the dead, the virgin birth, and the power of miracles. God's subjects might know his 'wisdom and power' from a study of the works of nature, but only through Revelation do we come to understand God's goodness and bounty, his particular care for his special creation, and his instructions for Christian living.[47] Revelation offered the clearest and easiest source of those moral rules prerequisite to salvation, especially for the labouring poor who lacked both the leisure and the necessary intellectual training for the science of morality. 'The greatest part cannot know', he admitted, 'and therefore they must believe.' And as he told Molyneux, 'as the Gospel provides a powerful set of morals, reason may be excused from the task of demonstration'.[48] Once it is established that Jesus was sent by God, all of his commands become law and 'there needs no other proof for the truth of what he says, but that he said it'.[49]

Locke's Christianity, and the guarantee of a Christian moral order on earth, was therefore impossible to realize without a place for Revelation, something the Deists would not accept. But in order to distinguish genuine Revelation from fancy or imagination, 'the Conceits of a warmed or over-weening Brain',[50] Locke concluded that the faculty of reason, God's special gift to men and women, must serve as the final referee of what was to be accepted as authentic. Just as the magistrate must rule according to the principles of reason, genuine Revelation will always conform to the rationality inherent in God's nature. Although Revelation might overrule 'the probable Conjectures of reason', this instrument of cognition plays an important role in Christianity by virtue of its capacity to evaluate communications that transcend the grasp of knowledge.[51] We accept Revelation on the strength of the testimony of others, and for Locke the accounts of the apostles were unimpeachable. Thus the evidence for the truth of Revelation was itself empirical in nature, much like other facts presented to us for our judgement.

One difficulty with this effort to place reason in the role of arbiter here is that Locke never defined what marks reason can take as criteria of genuine Revelation; in his eagerness to curb the excesses of religious enthusiasm he never specifically informed his audience how reason concludes that a particular Revelation is trustworthy or how it discriminates between the preternatural and mere delusion.[52] Nor did he ever work through the Bible in an effort to identify where revealed truths were to be found. What was important for Locke concerned the overall integrity of revealed truth at a time when Deists were marginalizing Revelation as an epistemological tool and declaring for the sufficiency of reason in all matters involving mankind's relationship with his Maker. He felt satisfied to establish the general principle of legitimacy for truths in Scripture which transcend reason, especially since those truths were to provide the guideposts for moral action and the shaping of the person.

While the charge of Socinianism was frequently made against Locke during the final decade of his life, only the irascible John Edwards accused him of being a Deist. The only plausible grounds for the reproach, and certainly not Edwards's intention, would rest in personal associations, wanted or otherwise, which Locke had with radical thinkers. John Toland, for example, boldly claimed Locke's *Essay* as the inspiration for his own radical religion of reason in *Christianity Not Mysterious*, while Anthony Collins, another influential Deist, became a close friend of Locke's during the final years of the latter's life. Locke clearly shared some things in common with Deism: a critical approach to Scripture, a renewed respect for reason as an instrument of investigation, the desire to simplify the requirements of the faith, and a distaste for coercion of any sort when matters of belief were under discussion. But there were significant differences as well, differences sometimes overlooked by later students of Locke. His affirmation of the fact that Revelation provided access to truths unavailable to reason, his acceptance of miracle in what was becoming an increasingly mechanistic universe, and, most crucially, his traditional anthropology or view of human nature, set Locke apart from the men who would have eagerly supplanted mystery, sin, and Revelation with the twin gifts of rationality and the full autonomy to merit eternal reward through good works alone.

The last issue, Locke's picture of human nature, is undoubtedly the most problematic in terms of elucidating the significance of his epistemology, and his religious outlook, for subsequent generations. The eighteenth century awarded Locke the posthumous distinction of having abolished the psychologically crippling myth of original sin and, by and large, this interpretation stands unassailed today.[53] There is much to be said on its behalf, especially if one considers the sheer power of Locke's polemic against innate ideas and his later commentary on the consequences of Adam's sin against the background of some 1500 years of Church teaching on the significance of the Fall. In Locke's day, both predestinarian Dissenters and latitudinarian champions of free will were agreed that the stain of Adam's disobedience continued to frustrate human efforts to enter into the kingdom of God.

Adam's arrogant desire to be like God, it was believed, would forever prevent his progeny from enjoying the fruits of eternal life without the special intervention, propitiation, and forgiveness of a providential Father. Adam, it was believed, represented all of humanity in his actions, thereby transmitting his personal guilt to all succeeding generations. John Tillotson, whose theology was about as far away from the harsh determinist perspective of the Puritan as any representative of the Restoration Church of England could be, nevertheless spoke with confidence about the deep depravity and constitutional sinfulness of humanity in the aftermath of the first sin.[54] The Christian story was simply meaningless without the assumption of obdurate sinfulness, of lifelong disobedience and a natural proclivity for that which was against God's dictate for humankind. Any challenge to this most primary of axioms was immediately associated with the amorphous, subterranean, sometimes vocal but always stealthy poison of Restoration Deism.

In 1675 Locke translated three of Pierre Nicole's *Essais de Morale*. Nicole was a Jansenist, but the goal of his *Essais* had been to mediate between Calvinism and Thomism. The pieces that Locke translated emphasized the need for individual sinners to cooperate with God's grace, to seek this grace in an effort to curb the self-centred will, and the requirement to divorce oneself from the vanity of the world's goods and to set one's sights on the permanent rewards in God's gift. Recently it has been argued that Locke most likely agreed with Nicole's pessimistic view of human nature at this point in his life, a view which insisted that God's assisting grace was imperative lest men's degenerate self-love overturn all moral rules. It is also likely that Locke accepted some form of original sin inherited from Adam, at least as far as incapacitating men for good without the help of divine assistance collaborating in their efforts. Only later, in the 1680s when Locke began a serious investigation of Scripture in order to rebut Sir Robert Filmer's account of government in the Old Testament, did he begin to question the traditional imputationist doctrine of the Fall as a taint inherited directly and permanently from the first man. Such an assault on original sin was essential if Locke were to undermine the linkage made by men like John Dryden, in his *Absalom and Achitophel* (1681) between divine right and hereditary monarchy and Adam's binding his posterity with the consequences of his actions. For if one were to accept the imputationist view of original sin, then the notion that one can inherit the sin of another could be made to serve the absolutist notion that political power is inherited by Adam's direct successors as well.[55] But when Locke did alter his views on the import of the traditional Fall story, when he rejected imputationism and began to write of the non-compulsory and habitual nature of sin, he remained firmly, and sadly, convinced of the fact that whatever the specific origins of human disobedience, most men lived in an extremely sinful state throughout the entire course of their lives.

Locke's dismissal of innate ideas in Book 2 of the *Essay*, coupled with his emphasis upon the importance of environmental factors in *Some Thoughts Concerning Education*, and with his rejection of Sir Robert Filmer's view of the consequences of the Fall, gave added significance to his contentious remarks in *The Reasonableness of Christianity*. Humankind has lost immortality thanks to Adam's disobedience, Locke observed, while no mention can be found in Scripture respecting the inheritance of guilt for the sin of another. For Locke there was no stain of original sin if by this term one meant shared responsibility for the particular transgression of Adam, a position confirmed by numerous Socinian authors that Locke had read during his years of exile in Holland. Any suggestion that men were somehow culpable for the actions of another destroyed for Locke the whole idea of divine justice and personal responsibility which he identified with the core of authentic Christianity. Each individual must be responsible for his own eternal fate; the child is born without inborn knowledge and the morally responsible 'person' is the product of external influences. The myth of the Fall, so central to the faith, and to absolutist political theory, yet so debilitating in its implications for the transformation of both individual and society, received its sharpest criticism in 1695 from a man who claimed a solid and lifelong attachment to the Christian story.

Perhaps the simplist way to grasp Locke's final position on original sin and his understanding of human nature in the aftermath of the Fall is to recall that the work of Christ in human form was to serve as a propitiation for sin, and that the sin in question was of a nature serious enough to exclude the possibility of humans ever meriting salvation as a debt owed by God in return for perfect obedience or righteousness. In other words, in *The Reasonableness*, Locke repeatedly stated his opposition to the Deist premise that humans, with the guidance of reason alone, could know and successfully follow the law of nature in a manner consistent with the divine requirement for complete obedience. Locke simply did not share the belief that any individual, no matter how dedicated, could merit the reward of eternal happiness without the saving work of Christ and the sustaining grace of the

Spirit. In this belief Locke shared company with all Christians who accepted the incomplete and inadequate nature of Adam's successors who were seeking the restoration of a blissful state and immortality. Only with the arrival of the second Adam in the person of Christ, and only under a new covenant whereby faith was graciously accepted in place of works of righteousness, would the potential of heavenly life be restored.

What human factor or set of factors, what empirical discovery had Locke made which was compelling enough to override the sanguine implications of his epistemology? The need for a redeemer, the admission that, in the end, salvation was not to be achieved without gratuitous assistance from the very being who had been offended repeatedly, stemmed from the fact that while no one inherited the guilt associated with Adam's great sin, everyone had become mortal in the wake of his disobedience, and mortality involved much more than the obvious point that all must die before real life begins. In particular, mortality entailed a loss of the mature use of reason available to Adam in Paradise. According to the Second Treatise, 'Adam was created the perfect man, his Body and Mind in full possession of their Strength and Reason.' The first sin had been made in the full knowledge of God's mandate. In the mortal postlapsarian state, on the other hand, no one enjoyed the 'full possession' of reason without proper instruction, without education.[56]

Locke's single doctrinal requirement before one could be considered a believing Christian was that one accept Christ as Messiah, and Messiahship involved, more than anything else, the salvation of ultimately undeserving subjects. The detailed description in the *Essay* of those factors that motivated men, the account of powerful emotions, innate dispositions, the desire for immediate happiness, and a natural self-centredness, all recalled Nicole's *Essais*, all counted against the performance of those moral rules which were potentially accessible by reason and set forth in Scripture. The mind was without ideas at birth, but the organism was constituted in such a way that natural penchants and predispositions, many of them at odds with the requirements of a Christian moral order, constantly disposed each human being toward a pattern of behaviour where only a very large reservoir of divine love and patience could override the destructive consequences of common thought and action. By 1695 Locke had certainly come to reject an original sin defined as guilt transmitted for offences committed by another, a definition central to Filmer's patriarchal politics, but he had left intact a more significant Christian anthropology which held that humans since the Fall were incapable of working out their salvation unassisted. The bare assertion that all ideas, and ultimately all knowledge, proceeded from sense experience gathered after birth, and in particular through the educational process, in no way reduced the significance of extraordinary help intended to remedy the consequences of man's natural tendency to violate God's law, the law of nature and reason. Locke's acceptance of grace and forgiveness was repugnant to the Deist sensibility.

The significance of Locke's commitment to a theology of grace where divine forgiveness follows the acceptance of Christ and the prosecution of a life in accordance with strict precepts, was lost upon nervous contemporaries who found it difficult to accept that anyone who would make all ideas, even the idea of God himself, to be the product of nothing more than bare experience, could in fact be an advocate for the faith, much less a self-styled defender of the traditional core truths. Nor could a man who placed reason at the heart of the religious enterprise and who limited knowledge to the external world be anything other than a Socinian, Deist, or Unitarian, terms of derision used freely and interchangeably in the late seventeenth century. Locke had little patience for such tendentious critics. In a letter written to an acquaintance in Utrecht soon after the appearance of the *Essay*, Locke stated that if his opponents 'are of those religious men, who when they can shew noe faults in his book can look into the heart of the author & there see flaws in the religion of him that writ it, though there be noe thing concerning religion in it, only because it is not suited to the systems they were taught I leave them to bethink themselves whether they are his disciples whose command it was, Judg not.'[57]

By the standards of the age Locke had strayed into heterodoxy by the 1690s. He had certainly come to reject the notion that all persons were born into a national church or that any church served as the exclusive conduit of saving grace. By the final decade of his life he probably embraced Unitarianism because he could not find the doctrine of the Trinity in Scripture, not because, as his critics alleged, of his attack on traditional definitions of substance in the *Essay*. He had remained silent on the question of the interregnum between death and resurrection for the same reason, and he had demurred at the prospect of the same body returning at the resurrection because the Pauline Epistles had been emphatic about the need for spiritualized bodies in the realm of incorruptibility. He had defined person not, as was the norm, as a mystical union of material body and immaterial soul, but in terms of individual consciousness of actions taken and acceptance of responsibility for those actions, because only with such a definition could one be held morally accountable in the next world. And he disputed the Augustinian doctrine of original sin, the fault of Adam communicated to posterity, both on account of its unscriptural nature, and just as importantly, because it propped up a system of patriarchal and authoritarian rule which had no place in Locke's vision for a free and responsible people. Anchoring his various critiques of orthodoxy in a personal exegesis of the Word of God, Locke transformed that text into a document of liberation and a licence for resistance to all forms of coercive rule in the century after his death. His minimalist Christianity, where the priesthood had no coercive or directive role, where the church community was a voluntary body, fostered both the freedom and the responsibility of individual believers. He was not confident that many men, thus liberated, would employ their new-found freedom in a search for and practice of life-saving morality. Enhancing the prospects for a life and character deserving of eternal reward would be the extraordinary task of the educator.

4
EDUCATION INTO HUMANITY

Coming from an Oxford-trained academic and member of an intellectual elite, Locke's dissent from the conventional norms of educational theory and practice represented yet another aspect of his larger project to redefine acceptable standards of authority in the late seventeenth century, to find a stable basis on which to guide thought and conduct. *Some Thoughts Concerning Education* (1693), his principal statement on educational matters, resulted from the confluence of a number of intellectual forces, not the least of which were his previous statements, voiced in the *Essay*, respecting the origin of ideas and the role of the mind active in the learning process. But equally as important to the development of his educational theory was an acute and prolonged observation of human behaviour in a variety of settings, including formal academic ones. Locke wished to discover the appropriate method of bringing the child into a mature use of reason because he was convinced that only through education would the youngster become a moral agent worthy of salvation. Education alone would make us truly human; it alone would restore the use of mature reason enjoyed by our first parents before the Fall. To leave the child in a state of untutored liberty, he maintained in *Two Treatises of Government*, was to thrust him out 'amongst brutes, and abandon him to a state as wretched, and as much beneath that of a Man, as theirs'.[1] Genuine freedom and self-mastery, secured through education into the constant use of reason, was for Locke a freedom to pursue salvation as well as being an essential prerequisite to objectives that were instrumental to salvation. Chief among these objectives was the formation of a political order by rational agents for the good of the wider community. The possession and employment of reason made possible the organization of political society without paternal rule.

Locke's credentials as an educator were quite unique in terms of his actual contact with young people, and this is especially true when one considers that he had no children of his own. While many of the other seventeenth-century manuals of instruction and advice convey a sense of formality and distance from particular life experiences, *Some Thoughts*, when taken together with Locke's many letters to and from friends respecting their children, abounds with advice anchored in direct empirical encounters and everyday observation. There is a concrete, practised quality to Locke's observations on childhood cognitive and emotional development, a familiarity with ordinary events and encounters in a household environment. Before writing the letters which became *Some Thoughts*, Locke had served for six years as a tutor *in loco parentis* at Oxford, instructed the future second Earl of Shaftesbury while living in the first Earl's London household, directed the education of Shaftesbury's seven grandchildren, cared for the son of Sir John Banks in France between 1677 and 1679, offered his advice on childrearing matters to a number of his friends, and lived for extended periods in two households (Benjamin Furly's home in Amsterdam and Damaris Masham's home at Oates) where young children were being raised. When he stated in *Some Thoughts* that children, almost as soon as they are born, and certainly before they can speak, cry to have their wills and to dominate others, he was speaking as a man who had witnessed these traits on a number of occasions, and not only on the basis of abstract, *a priori* theory. And when he observed that these two traits constituted the 'Roots of almost all the Injustice and Contention, that so disturb Humane Life', he may not have been affirming a traditional Adam-based notion of original sin where each person inherits the guilt attached to the first transgression, but he was nevertheless describing a natural propensity which, if left unchecked, would overturn every tenet of natural law as Locke understood them.[2]

As we noted in the previous chapter, the most recent scholarship in this area has concluded that Locke broke with the imputationist understanding of original sin whereby Adam represented all of humanity. Rather, it is now claimed, all that Locke agreed was forfeited by the first sin was immortality and the pleasures of Eden. If this conclusion is allowed, however, we are still left to explain why children seek to dominate others from the earliest age. If children have no propensity toward evil, then why did Locke emphasize the overriding need for carefully supervised education into the exercise of rationality? With no innate moral truths to guide us, no natural inclination to the good, only education stood between the individual's sinful propensity and God's judgement based on conduct in this life. Virtue is harder to acquire than a knowledge of the world, Locke believed, and the non-rational, precipitous, self-absorbed side of human nature, if left unchecked, invariably leads to sin against a benevolent and forgiving Creator.[3] The person who fails to learn and then to obey the rule of reason quite simply rejects his Maker's claim to his obedience and jeopardizes his prospects for eternal happiness.

Locke began composing the letters which would, after much revision, become *Some Thoughts* in July of 1684 while living in Holland. A distant relative and friend, Edward Clarke of Chipley, Somerset, requested advice on the education of his eldest son and heir, Edward Jr, then ten years of age. The letters continued until 1688, by which time Locke had assembled more than enough material for a useful book. Additional letters from Locke on educational matters arrived at Chipley until just before Locke's death in 1704. In February 1688 Locke told Clarke that with every letter he sent he hoped to conclude his advice, 'yet it is seldom very long before I find reason for some addition'.[4] The text of *Some Thoughts* was essentially completed by 1690, but Locke's penchant for revision, together with his timidity about publication, delayed the book's appearance for another two years. Like most of his major works, *Some Thoughts* was printed anonymously, as Locke confided to his friend William Molyneux that his recommendations 'have run me so far out of the common road and practice' that he wished to avoid whatever controversy might ensue.[5]

In certain respects, Locke's nervousness might seem misplaced, for *Some Thoughts* advocated a programme of intellectual and moral enrichment entirely in keeping with the spirit of other popular seventeenth-century manuals on education. Locke read widely in a number of fields, and his final library indicates that he was familiar with current work on educational theory and practice. Following a tradition in large measure established by Thomas Eliot in his 1531 *The Boke Named the Governor*, continued in the seventeenth century by authors like Henry Peacham and Jean Gailhard, both of whom published books titled *The Compleat Gentleman*, and echoed by contemporary theorists such as Obadiah Walker (*Of Education, Especially of Young Gentlemen*, 1673) and Stephen Penton (*The Guardian's Instruction*, 1688), Locke stressed the malleability of youth together with the importance of character formation over the mastery of specific content or curriculum.[6]

All of these works, Locke's included, were designed mainly with the gentleman's son in mind, the future public person whose example would presumably set the moral tone for the nation. Gentlemen landowners made up about 2 per cent of the entire English population of some 5 million, and since these 15,000 fortunate individuals were not obliged to engage in physical labour, service to one's neighbours was thought to be their natural responsibility. Unfortunately, in Locke's opinion, the gentry had become far too complacent and self-indulgent, with many living beyond their means, mismanaging their estates, and ignoring their natural duties as leaders in society.[7] Piety and morality, the conventional Christian virtues, all find pride of place in books devoted to the proposition that social and political order are stable only where the character of the elite is in harmony with the dictate of God's law or reason. Outward appearances, while important in maintaining a sense of decorum, were irrelevant to the fate of a people whose long-term health could only be assured by proper education into virtue, virtue which was theirs not by nature but rather by design, by deliberate effort.[8] Everyone must, at some point in their lives, be trusted to govern themselves, Locke believed, 'and he that is a good, a vertuous and able Man, must be made so within' by habits 'woven into the very Principles of his Nature'.[9] Goodness and virtue, in other words, were not native to mankind.

Recently, it has been suggested that a proposal made by Locke as a member of the Board of Trade in 1697 calling for the establishment of 'working schools' for the poor extended his ideas for educational reform to the labouring classes. In that paper, which was part of a larger recommendation for reform of England's Poor Laws, Locke refers to the children aged 3 to 14 as 'scholars' and the managers of the workhouses as 'schoolmasters or dames'. But there is no mention made of any formal education to be undertaken in the workhouses beyond the trades of spinning and knitting, and there is certainly no call for the type of direct tutorial instruction that Locke believed was imperative if a boy or girl were to develop habits of virtue and the practice of self-denial necessary to rational living. In fact the sole advantage of the working school scheme in terms of the moral development of the child lay in the requirement that youngsters be in attendance at church on Sunday, 'whereby they may be brought into some sense of religion'. Locke did indicate in a separate paper that all persons should be exposed to a regular course of physical labour and he believed that 'the man of manual labour' should devote at least three hours each day 'on his minde in thought and reading'. Such a course would free the poor 'from that horid ignorance and brutality to which the bulke of them is now every where given up'. But his plan for workhouses makes no specific mention of how such a routine would be undertaken, contains no discussion of curricular content, and offers no suggestions respecting pedagogic method in the workhouse setting. James Tully's contention that the 'working schools' proposal was designed to create individuals who would be habituated to labour and docility seems closer to the mark of Locke's intentions, especially given Locke's overriding political interest in maintaining an ordered society for the protection of property rights.[10]

Locke's book on education differed from most manuals not only in its refusal to place curricular matters at the centre of the learning process, but also in its total absence of the usual nostrums regarding appropriate religious content. The reader of *Some Thoughts* finds no sectarian agenda, no ecclesiological preferences, no formulae on specific prayers or private reflection. The clergyman John Edwards, who as we have seen was one of Locke's most vitriolic detractors, had little difficulty in linking Locke's silence on the place of religious instruction in the learning process with Locke's Socinian and atheistical intentions in the *Essay* and in *The Reasonableness of Christianity*. But even if we discount the tendentious accusations of a deeply troubled man like Edwards, one does not have to read extensively in the educational literature of the period to recognize that the inculcation of very definite religious values normally takes pride of place in the daily programme. James Talbott's *The Christian School-Master* (1707) published three years after Locke's death, was typical of the genre in appending a collection of prayers for various occasions. Locke wrote that the foundation of virtue depends upon 'a true Notion of God' being imprinted on the child's mind early, but young boys and girls should not be made 'too Curious in their Notions about a Being, which all must acknowledge incomprehensible'. He recommended acts of devotion to God 'suitable to their Age and Capacity' and later offered advice on what parts of the Bible provide 'easy and plain moral Rules' for young children, most of whom, he believed, learned nothing from the current practice of reading Scripture by sequential chapters. Being made aware of 'the plainest Fundamental Parts' of Scripture at the outset, children should then be encouraged to read more difficult parts, always avoiding commentaries by men 'prepossess'd by Systems and Analogies'.[11]

Some Thoughts Concerning Education also breaks new ground in its endorsement of physical labour and commerce as undertakings appropriate for the educated gentleman. 'I would have him learn a Trade, a Manual Trade; nay, two or three, but one more particularly.' Husbandry, gardening, iron- and woodworking, and other tasks not only improve health, but enhance dexterity and personal discipline. Keeping good accounts will enable the gentleman to preserve his estate and, by implication, will enhance the economic well-being of the nation. In each of these endeavours Locke stresses a work ethic and skills base very much in harmony with the emerging agrarian and commercial capitalism of the late seventeenth century.[12] More significantly, he linked industriousness with God's goodness since physical labour strengthened the body and promoted virtue. Virtue and industry, he thought, were 'as constant companions on the one side as vice and idleness are on the other'.[13] Most persons lived on the very margins of self-sufficiency in pre-industrial England, and everyone was expected to contribute to the production of the nation's goods if the economy were to advance. Eschewing all social distinctions, Locke's list of those who posed a burden to society included beggars, 'Gamesters', 'Retainers to Gentry', 'Multitudes of Lawyers', but above all 'soldiers in pay'.[14]

The question of whether or not Locke believed that the child at birth was naturally disposed to one set of behaviours over another has been the subject of some controversy over the past few years. The emphasis in Book 2 of the *Essay* on the *tabula rasa* has had a profound impact on how later commentators have viewed Locke's understanding of the issue. Generally, most scholars have denied that Locke entertained any attachment to the Christian notion of the Adamic Fall and the subsequent taint of original sin, and thus any suggestion that the untutored child would naturally engage in immoral behaviour underestimated the centrality of Locke's epistemology for his theory of learning and action. Locke did indicate, after all, that parents should be cautious lest they 'instill Principles of Vice into them', implying that bad example alone led the youngster astray.[15] At the opening of *Some Thoughts* he observed that 'all the Men we meet with, Nine Parts of Ten are what they are, Good or Evil, useful or not, by their Education', strongly suggesting that no specific nature could be attached to the infant at birth. We should be cautious, however, about identifying Locke's theory of the *tabula rasa* with a specific view of natural dispositions at the outset of life. Bishop William King of Dublin, who was one of the first to comment critically on Locke's denial of innate ideas in the *Essay*, and a man who accepted the traditional Adamic Fall story, could nevertheless confirm without hesitation that

'we came into the World without any actual Knowledge of outward
things; our Minds were certainly, as to them, once like clean Paper, in
which nothing is yet written'. And there were others who could
subscribe to the image of the mind at birth as an empty cabinet and
still maintain a deep scepticism regarding man's essential nature.
Richard Allestree's *Whole Duty of Man* and *The Gentleman's Calling*,
both books assigned by Locke to his undergraduates at Christ Church
in the early 1660s, emphasized the malleable nature of children's
minds despite the consequences of the Fall. And Jean Gailhard,
writing in 1678, thought that 'The nature of Youth for the most part
is like Wax by the fire' even though his inward nature was 'naturally
corrupt, namely the mind darkened, and so unable to discern true
from false, the will and affections deprav'd and prone to evil'.[16]
Unchecked natural passions, what one modern scholar has called
'the corrupt passions released by the Fall', provided another important
determinant of behaviour from infancy onward.[17] These innate appetites had to be disciplined before the mind barren of content at birth
could be instilled with ideas conducive to the type of rational thought
and action mandated by God's intentions for his special creation.

In both the more famous *Essay* and in *Some Thoughts* Locke takes
considerable pains to stress the individual peculiarities of each child,
the unique and often troublesome humours, tempers, and tendencies of
mind, all of which are wholly beyond the power of voluntary instruction to completely amend or refashion. It is not insignificant that he
concluded the work on education by highlighting the fact that 'a
thousand other things' not treated in the book need consideration due
to 'the various Tempers, different Inclinations, and particular De-
faults, that are to be found in Children'.[18] At best the tutor must
recognize these innate character traits or natural dispositions and work
with them in the hope of amendment for the sake of forming a moral
'person' who accepts responsibility for his actions. Certainly Locke was
not blind to the power of non-rational and unconscious forces in the
thought and action of his contemporaries. This was obvious as early as
1659 when he wrote that the passions, the brutish part of human
nature, often govern our thoughts and actions.[19] These words were,
admittedly, written at a time when the Cromwellian experiment was
coming to an inglorious end, when Locke welcomed the return of the
monarchy as the best means of curbing the ignorant enthusiasm of
Protestant sectaries. But 20 years later, in the midst of the Exclusion
controversy, he reaffirmed this basic outlook when he confided in a
journal entry that 'The three great things that govern mankind are

reason, passion and superstition. The first governs a few, the two last share the bulk of mankind and possess them in their turns. But superstition most powerfully produces the greatest mischief.' And the mischief would not be abated until the goals of education were redefined and a new approach to instruction undertaken.

In the chapter 'Of Power' in the *Essay*, a chapter added to the second edition of the work in 1694, Locke appeared to indicate that every individual, regardless of educational opportunity, was capable of restraining his immediate appetites and passions in the decision-making process, 'for what he can do before a Prince, or a great Man, he can do alone, or in the presence of God, if he will'. Locke later elaborated on this statement, although he never incorporated these additional passages into the *Essay*. Observing the widespread brutishness, dissolution, and irrationality of his fellows, he posited three explanations as to why such individuals did not pause to consider the implications of their actions for their future happiness. In the first place it appeared that both rich and poor alike were too apt to indulge the passions of youth and by encouraging a contrary habit, had denied their offspring 'the use and exercise of reflection'. In the second instance, and perhaps more seriously, men of leisure who are afforded the opportunity for intellectual improvement have, through bad company and poor principles, come to 'cast away the thought and beliefs of another world as a fiction of politicians and divines conspiring together to keep the world in awe, and to impose on weak minds'. For the man who has abandoned belief in heaven and hell, Locke claims, virtue is a stranger. Finally there are those who are not irreligious by intellectual habit, but whose already dissolute lives convince them that their prospects for happiness in a future state are not good, and who thereby convince themselves to secure all the pleasure they can while alive.[20] None of these additional reflections to the chapter 'Of Power' suggests that mere self-determination on the part of the unwary child is enough to overcome the attractions of immediate pleasure which present themselves at every moment of waking experience. Without actualizing the potential rational nature through deliberate conditioning, the prospect of a distant reward or punishment, even though it be unending in nature, would not influence behaviour. Education was a basic prerequisite to salvation.

According to Locke, children do have a basic uniform nature, which is rational, and a God-given potential, which is mastery and self-definition, but the power of reason – what Locke referred to in the First Treatise of Government as the 'Image of God' in humankind –

must be developed, brought out, through the often painstaking process of education and socialization. Children have no internal moorings without adult guidance and supervision; each child must develop the capacity to distinguish good from evil, to suspend judgement and deliberate, and to act in accordance with the larger ends of truth and probity. In the Second Treatise Locke had made it clear that the child 'has not Understanding of his own to direct his Will' and parents 'must prescribe to his Will, and regulate his Actions'.[21] But even if educated into the principles of virtue and morality, in the end the 'rational' individual still has the final freedom to disregard the promptings of reason. In other words, habits can be inculcated, but each person must freely submit to the dictate of reason and resulting virtue. The student must be habituated to stop and think before accepting any proposition as true, but he is free not to reflect if he so chooses. Ultimately, as Peter Schouls has argued quite recently, no individual can entirely escape responsibility for their actions by claiming that they were the product of a bad environment, for no environment is totally irresistible.

Locke considered this power to deliberate, to reflect on what potential actions were most apt to forward our greatest happiness, as an enormous responsibility and obligation that we owe to God as rational Christians. He stated plainly and directly in the *Essay* that 'a man may justly incur punishment, though it be certain that in all the particular actions that he will, he does, and necessarily does will that, which he then judges to be good'. By a too hasty choice he often follows the wrong measures of good and evil; unfortunately for those who act precipitously 'The eternal Law and Nature of things must not be alter'd to comply with his ill-order'd choice'.[22] In the same opening paragraph of *Some Thoughts* where Locke underscored the role of education, he also reaffirmed individual autonomy by stating that 'Men's Happiness or Misery is most part of their own making'. To rely on reason alone, and to act according to its direction, one must reject all of the beliefs, habits and practices of one's cultural setting, all religious, political, educational authorities. One's culture must be consistently transcended, and, as he states this epistemic autonomy in the *Essay*, 'Reason must be our last Judge and Guide in every Thing'.[23] This alone was the prerequisite to freedom and self-mastery.

The cultivation of reason, however, was merely one stage in the educational process. As we suggested in chapter 2, a larger and more difficult task faced the skilled tutor once the student's potential for rational thought had been awakened. Locke had stated in the *Essay* that what motivates people to action is, above all else, the ever-present desire to secure terrestrial pleasure and the parallel urge to avoid pain; he called these innate practical (moral) principles. And happiness 'is the utmost Pleasure we are capable of, and Misery the utmost Pain'.[24] In other words, reason is not a sufficient motive to moral behaviour; what we perceive as being in the interest of our happiness, rather than what we know to be the good, will determine our action in every case. Individuals, unfortunately, 'may have a clear view of good, great and confessed good, without being concern'd for it, or moved by it, if they think they can make up their happiness without it'.[25] At the centre of *Some Thoughts* is the conviction that the satisfaction of immediate pleasures must be avoided, curbed and regulated by the voice of reason, because more often than not the pleasures near at hand are those at odds with the Christian, life-saving virtues. The great principle of all virtue and all human worth, he asserted, resides in the fact that a person 'is able to deny himself his own Desires, cross his own Inclinations, and purely follow what Reason directs as best, tho' the appetite lean the other way'.[26] In this his claim merely echoed the reservations of earlier commentators such as Edward Hyde, Earl of Clarendon, who observed that 'Children are capable of learning what is bad, before they can understand the Reason why any thing is good, or why the other is bad, and yet having learned it, retain it afterwards in spite of all Reason.' The youngster who is not able to master his appetites and inclinations, Locke insisted, 'wants the true Principle of Vertue and Industry; and is in Danger never to be good for any thing'.[27] Included in 'any thing', of course, is the greatest goal that humankind sets for itself, the reward for conduct becoming the faith one embraces in private and public profession.

As we have already seen, Locke never provided his readers with a well-defined list of universal moral rules derived solely from the law of nature, but in *Some Thoughts* it is clear that the qualities which he associated with the moral person were the conventional and centuries-old Christian ones. John Yolton has assembled a list of these qualities in his recent critical edition of Locke's book on education, where humility, industry, civility, generosity, modesty, self-control, and self-restraint are shown to be some of the more important, and familiar, features to be internalized by the virtuous person. According to Locke's natural law theory, each of these qualities had their foundation in reason and in God's will (the second table of the Decalogue), yet all of them had to be learned; each child had to see that the observance of these qualities would provide a key part of the long-term happiness which all sought to secure. And that task was a considerable one, especially in light of the many immediate pleasures that presented themselves to the untutored child. For young people, 'Their want of Judgement makes them stand in need of Restraint and Discipline', and the younger the child the more crucial it was to bring their disorderly appetites under restraint. Locke would have agreed with Clarendon's view that 'It is a general and fatal Mistake, that we believe Children incapable of Instruction till they have such a Proportion of Reason as to understand what is good and what is ill.'[28] When little, children who have no criteria by which to judge their many experiences must be made to 'look upon their Parents as their Lords, their Absolute Governors, and, as such, stand in awe of them'.[29] Here was a view first expressed in the *Two Treatises*, and while it did not lead Locke to an acceptance of corporal punishment (in fact he, like John Aubrey before him, thought that severity of punishment did great harm) it nevertheless proceeded from Locke's deep worry that a lack of discipline would end in the child's constant violation of the laws of nature set by God.[30]

In the *Essay*, Locke had observed that there were three sets of laws which regulated human conduct: divine law, civil law, and the law of reputation or opinion. He readily acknowledged that for most of human history the third law, the 'Law of fashion', had provided the most powerful precepts by which people had comported themselves.[31] While at one level such an admission might be looked upon as an indication of how unreasonable and short-sighted people of all ages might be, Locke attempted to turn this difficult situation to his advantage by alerting the prospective tutor to the overwhelming power of cultivating good habits. For Locke the key to inculcating this willingness to forgo the satisfaction of immediate pleasures lay in the proper management of people's natural desire for approbation, the approval and applause of their contemporaries. Some of Pierre Nicole's *Essais de Moral*, translated by Locke back in the 1670s, had emphasized the view that people's actions were largely determined by the opinions and norms of others; that the approval of immediate peers always confirmed one's own high opinion of himself or herself. Locke forcefully enlisted this doctrine of approbativeness in the cause of Christian virtue in *Some Thoughts*. The child's constant desire for approval could be used by the skilled tutor in order to induce good behaviour. Example rather than precept, approval instead of rebuke; these were the keys to harnessing otherwise unseemly and egotistic qualities to the cause of universal morality.

By making the child ashamed of his faults and errors, the tutor could bring his charge to act in accordance with the principles of reason. 'If you can once get into Children a love of Credit, and an apprehension of Shame and Disgrace, you have put into them the true Principle, which will constantly work, and incline them to the right.'[32] Locke always insisted that the real measure of virtue was the extent of a person's voluntary submission to God's law in light of the promise of reward that is given to him, but shaping right conduct on the basis of egocentric reputation was the next best thing to obedience on the grounds of a rational understanding of divine law, and an important asset in the pursuit of real virtue. The longing for favour which Christian commentators from the time of St Augustine had decried as ethically suspect was viewed by Locke as a means of creating genuine virtue in the child. Locke's frankness here, his admission that the child's selfish interests must be harnessed and manipulated into worthwhile channels, gave his work a pragmatic appeal lacking in more formal treatises on education.

Aside from the dissenting academies which emerged in the wake of the Clarendon Code, institutional education during Locke's day was centred on a traditional scholastic curriculum, with most emphasis being placed upon the subjects of the medieval *trivium* (Latin and Greek grammar, logic and rhetoric). Locke thought it strange that parents had a greater concern that their children master 'the languages of the Greeks and Romans' before they had learned to be persons of good character.[33] The practice of the disputation, where propositions were defended and attacked in Latin, was embraced as the key exercise in the assessment of scholastic ability. Locke also believed that one approach to education, and in particular the uniformity of the classroom format, was impractical given that no two people had the same dispositions or aptitudes. Reflecting on his own dissatisfaction with his education at Westminster and at Christ Church, he turned to the tutorial model as the ideal educational arrangement. Even the best-intentioned instructor in a formal school, having his students for but part of the day, cannot 'instruct them Successfully in any thing, but their Books: The forming of their minds and Manners requiring constant Attention, and particular Application to every single Boy, which is impossible in a numerous Flock'.[34]

Only under the personal and private circumstances of the tutor–student relationship could the educator get to know the natural temper of the child's mind. No two children being alike, each person's mind having 'some peculiarity' that distinguishes it from all others, the sensitive tutor was to devote all of his attention to the character formation of his single charge. Instruction must begin at the earliest possible age, and it must take account at the outset of any natural biases in the youngster. The standards which Locke set for the tutor were extremely high, and he advised his readers to think of an investment in the best tutor available as the wisest expenditure of money one could make during any point in the child's life. The tutor, in fact, was key to Locke's plan for a new educational ideal, and it would be less than fair to say that each tutor faced anything other than a massive and demanding task. For while children are potentially reasonable, they are from an early age bombarded by the culture's established fashion, custom, opinion, wrong notions, and ill habits. Bringing them into reason involved freeing them from whatever received opinion they might entertain. With so many persons all too willing to accept unexamined and received opinions, the tutor must be diligent in preventing the child from falling into the same lazy trap. Too many individuals, by long custom and education, have had established prejudices 'insinuated into their unwary, as well as un-biass'd Understandings'.[35] And erroneous principles instilled into the young are rarely re-examined in adulthood, especially when 'the desire of Esteem, Riches, or Power' makes men willingly subscribe to the belief systems of those in a position to reward their ambitions.[36]

The ideal tutor must not only be a person of upright Christian character who can gently and without force guide the student towards virtue through example and the formation of habit, but he must also be willing and able to encourage the student, at the appropriate stage of intellectual and moral development, to question even the wisdom of the prescribed curriculum itself. Instilling virtue, creating the will to be good, may be the hardest part of education, but knowing when to let the pupil challenge the assumptions guiding his entire Lockean programme is consequential as well. Autonomy and freedom can only be assured when the 'person', acknowledging responsibility for his thought and action, and guided by natural reason, begins to evaluate all knowledge claims – including those put forward by the tutor – for himself. Good education does not seek to impose truths, indeed its encouragement of a questioning attitude may result in the student's rejection of his culture's standards if, upon reflection, his reason finds them to be without foundation.[37]

The job of the educator, then, was to help the young person to see that his greatest pleasure, and his most lasting happiness, would be secured through an obedience to the rule of reason. It was due to this fact that Locke placed the qualities of 'Sobriety, temperance, tenderness, diligence and discretion' above scholarly attainment in a prospective tutor. The tutor must be convinced that children would never hunger after righteousness before they had been made to feel uneasy at its absence, until they had learned to desire virtuous living as the most direct means to personal pleasure. 'Change but a Man's view of these things; let him see, that Virtue and Religion are necessary to his Happiness', and the ethical hedonism at the core of Locke's mature moral theory would be made serviceable to society. But if the tutor failed in his efforts to raise the child's desires to this elevated plane, he would narrow the chances of the child ever securing the rewards of a rational life. Anyone 'that will not be so far a rational Creature, as to reflect seriously upon infinite Happiness and Misery, must needs condemn himself, as not making that use of his Understanding he should.'[38] Success for the tutor comes when his charge is convinced that both temporal and eternal happiness – genuine control over our destiny – proceeds from the life of reason. Free from prejudice, unmoved by custom and tradition, hardened against current fashion or opinion, the autonomous individual consistently eschews immediate desires for the biblical promise of lasting joy.

Although Locke devoted the majority of his directions to the formation of Christian character, shaping the individual who practises virtue by habit and not by rules or out of fear of punishment, he did not entirely neglect specific subject matter appropriate for the gentleman who would eventually take his place in the public life of his country. Reading, writing, spelling, and languages were to be integrated in his programme, making the study of foreign language not exclusively an extended exercise in grammar. Geography was important as an early subject because children loved to learn by seeing. The basics of arithmetic introduced the child to 'the first sort of abstract reasoning' and prepared him for the practical business of everyday life. Rhetoric, logic, natural science, and law are introduced later in the process, while chronology complements the study of geography and history.

The role of history in Locke's proposed curriculum is of special interest due not least to the fact that priestly and princely authority, together with the weight of tradition in religious thought, provided the bulwarks of the intellectual *ancien régime* that Locke was working to overturn. Locke abhorred the delight many children take in seeing other living things in pain and maintained that it was an execrable habit learned from adults. In particular, most formal and informal discussion of history was unnecessarily centred on 'Fighting and Killing: And the Honour and Renoun, that is bestowed on Conquerors (who for the most part are but the great Butchers of Mankind)'. By such a distorted review of the past children 'come to think Slaughter the laudable Business of Mankind, and the most Heroick of Vertues'.[39] Sixteen years before the publication of *Some Thoughts* he had observed that the study of history might provide a man with entry into the world of the learned, but would do little to advance true knowledge.[40] In place of the anti-social qualities encouraged by the history now taught, the guardian and parents must be careful to instil a 'more natural Temper of Benignity and Compassion, not least in the history curriculum'. History, if presented correctly, is 'the great Mistress of Prudence and Civil Knowledge'. It should both teach and delight the reader, preparing him for a constructive life by informing him of the origins and development of societies and the rights of men.[41] The lessons of history, for example, indicated that all governments that were established in peace, 'had their beginning laid on that foundation, and were made by the Consent of the People'.[42] While *Some Thoughts* recommended Latin history, English history, and biblical history, in 'Some Thoughts Concerning Reading and Study for a Gentleman' (1703), Locke indicated that the history of one's own country was essential for an understanding of the art of government. He recommended James Tyrrell's *General History of England* (1697–1700) for this purpose, doubtless because this work stressed the crucial role of the legislative branch in the English experience; earlier, as a tutor at Oxford, he had assigned Jean Bodin's *Method for the Easy Comprehension of History* (1566) to his students, a book committed to situating events in their proper, separate and unique temporal context.[43] According to Locke, a knowledge of men was to be had first (and not surprisingly) from direct experience and secondly from a study of the past.[44]

Locke's advice to others about the importance of reading history to the development of an appropriate critical sense respecting the political condition of one's own nation is interesting in light of the fact that some contemporary scholars see Locke as lacking a historical sense himself. Unlike the philosophers Hobbes before him and Hume after him, Locke neither wrote a history nor based his politics on the history of England.[45] J.G.A. Pocock has observed that Locke's goal in *Two Treatises* was to write the first 'nonhistorical theory of politics' in the early modern period.[46] A large part of Locke's reluctance to use history was due, quite obviously, to his conviction that the rules and events of the past should by no means define what is just or right under present conditions. This he stated quite emphatically in *Two Treatises*, where, we shall see, he attempted to ground legitimate government in the law of nature.[47] Similarly, his epistemology was distinctly at odds with any notion of truth emanating solely from precedent or authority. And he also warned about the varied employment of words over time. In Book 3 of the *Essay*, he discussed how difficult it was to understand the exact meaning of words used by earlier generations, how 'different Notions, Tempers, Customs, Ornaments, and Figures of Speech . . . influenced the signification of their Words then, though to us now they are lost and unknown'.[48] He cited as an example of this the many conflicting interpreters of the Old and New Testaments. The word of God may be infallibly true, but our understanding of it is too often plagued by doubt and uncertainty. In the *Paraphrase* Locke approached St Paul's letters fully aware of the historical problems associated with the use of the Greek language to communicate ideas previously found only in Hebrew or Arabic, not to mention the difficulties associated with Paul's 'Stile and Temper'. In order to understand Paul's meaning, repeated reading of each epistle, 'with a close Attention to the Tenour of the Discourse' was absolutely essential. Locke emphasized a critical approach to the understanding of language which was focal to the advancement of modern historical knowledge.[49]

Despite these important cautions, however, Locke believed that if the child had previously 'well-settled in his mind the principles of morality, and knows how to make a judgement on the actions of men', and if he were alerted to the cultural and linguistic conventions unique to the period under treatment, then the study of the past became one of the most useful tools that the student could possess. In a letter of 1697 to Cary Mordaunt, Countess of Peterborough, regarding the education of her son, he reiterated that while familiarity with the past was 'one of the most necessary studys' for a member of the ruling elite, the study of morality should accompany all such undertakings.[50] Only then could the young man profit from past examples of virtue and rational conduct. To read history without this preliminary moral foundation was to find oneself without guideposts in distinguishing between the capriciousness and violence of most men in the past and the remnant of good in those who sought to ameliorate the human condition. Working from such a foundation, on the other hand, the student would be able to 'learn to think of men as they are', to see the rise of opinions from 'slight and sometimes shameful' origins, to be warned against 'the cheats and rogueries' of the world. He would also be prepared to distinguish between the fact that most early governments were under the administration of one man, but that 'almost all

Monarchies, near their Original, have been commonly, at last upon occasion, Elective'.[51] The 'plain historical' method employed in the *Essay* involved both the search for origins and the need for precision if the inaccurate readings of the past and the erroneous applications of the present were to be redressed.

In pressing relentlessly for a radical individualism in the learning process, in preparing the youngster for freedom by insisting upon the need to examine all knowledge claims, Locke was not endorsing epistemological subjectivism, nor did he accept any sort of cultural relativism. In fact, his methodological and epistemological individualism, borrowed from Descartes, sought to overcome the relativism of belief conditioned by specific cultural epochs. His belief that truth is always the same regardless of historical, social or cultural conditions, founded on his Christian natural law ethic, was articulated throughout his career. Locke had read widely in travel books and journals about peoples around the globe, and his ethnographic references from these sources can be found in many of his notebooks. 'The Americans are not all born with worse Understandings than the Europeans' he insisted in the *Conduct*, nor are the children of poor countrymen who are provided with education; variety of attainment and outlook was due to the 'different scope that has been given to their understandings to range in, for the gathering up of information, and furnishing their heads with ideas'.[52] Fashion and education – social environment – alone put the differences between people, obscuring the mandate of the law of nature or reason. This conviction by itself distinguished Locke from contemporary theorists of natural hierarchy. Truth is not relative to time or place for Locke because of his belief in the basic uniformity of human nature, a rational, egalitarian human nature. In a manner not altogether unlike Descartes, Locke believed that the individual pursuit of truth guided by infallible reason would yield broad consensus amidst the heterogeneity of cultures, just as Luther and the earliest reformers had hoped, one century before Descartes, that individual biblical exegesis, guided by the illuminated conscience, would generate the one true meaning of the unencumbered text.[53] God, the author of reason, provides the objective assurance of our rational certitude. And that certitude, based on the employment of critical reason, was humankind's best hope for the just society, one deserving of divine favour. 'It is a duty we owe to God', he claimed in his essay 'Of Study', 'to have our minds constantly disposed to entertain and receive truth wheresoever we meet with it' even if its appearance may be displeasing to some.[54]

Locke's book on education was well received upon its appearance in 1693. Like the *Two Treatises*, the letters to Edward Clarke which made up *Some Thoughts Concerning Education* emphatically rejected the patriarchal claim that children were at the arbitrary and complete command of their parents, just as subjects in civil society are not at the disposal of their prince. Parents are obliged to educate, not to master. Children may not be born into a state of equality with adults, but they are born to it. *Some Thoughts* reasserted the position introduced in *Two Treatises* that the rule of parents ' 'tis but a temporary one', while the law of nature demanded that parents nourish, preserve and educate their offspring.[55] Procreation is not the source of parental power because God, not man, is the maker of children. 'They who say the Father gives life to his Children, are so dazzled with the thoughts of Monarchy, that they do not, as they ought, remember God, who is the Author and Giver of Life; 'Tis in him alone we live, move, and have our Being.' And that being, Locke insisted, was designed for specific ends separate from the mundane aspirations of the head of a household. Parents must inform the minds of children until reason has matured, at which point the child becomes a free man and the equal of his mother and father.[56] All are born free, and all are born rational, 'not that we have actually the Exercise of either; Age that brings one, brings with it the other too'.[57] The audience for *Some Thoughts* was presumably receptive to the idea of putting the acquisition of Christian character ahead of curricular content, of acknowledging the inherent right of their offspring to freedom. And Locke's commonsense approach to learning devoid of corporal punishment doubtless contributed to a new view of childhood where the love of learning could be instilled by engaging the child's fascination with the new. Important as well were Locke's opening sections on the health of the body, and his advice regarding recreation and exercise, for in the view of the physician-author a robust body is best able 'to obey and execute the Orders of the Mind'.[58]

Locke's mature position on the place of education in the lives of his countrymen was informed in no small part by the overriding fact of human partiality and selfish, misdirected passion, qualities which had repeatedly frustrated the good faith efforts of reasonable men to fashion an orderly polity, a comprehensive and tolerant church, a better approach to knowledge and the amelioration of the human condition. His exile in Holland had afforded him abundant time to write, to work into final form the great texts for which he has been celebrated. But it was an involuntary exile, a forced exclusion prompted by the men of partiality who would abridge the natural God-given rights of an entire people for their own debased and sinful ends. There was little likelihood that the cycle of cruelty sponsored by religious intolerance and political repression would exit the European scene anytime soon so long as education was defined as the mastery of inherited norms and standards. The past 2000 years of bad principles and faulty logic had effectively eliminated personal autonomy in moral and political affairs. It was, more than anything else, these inherited principles which were holding men in paths of thought and conduct antithetical to the mandate of universal reason, God's mandate, the mandate of liberation and, in the end, salvation. Only a few had been bold enough to test and to reject the imposed order, the undemocratic epistemology, and their fate throughout history had not been a pleasant one. By making formal education a part of the larger process of socialization whereby virtuous citizens can act responsibly to preserve their individual freedoms, Locke viewed his ideas of education as contributing in an immediate way to the implementation of the method discussed in the *Essay*. The focus on the individual, and on the goal of liberating the individual from a slavish reliance upon the conventions of the day, stands at the heart of both the *Essay* and *Some Thoughts*. Knowledge of the past may assist us in that quest for autonomy, but it can never take the place of our own personal enlightenment, our own refusal to accept subject status without consent. Above all, Locke's educational writings emphasize the fusion of virtue with the dictate of reason, and the conjunction of reason with the Christian graces. Knowledge and action built upon the cornerstone of virtue are to be rewarded with prosperity here and eternal favour hereafter. No memorization of creeds, no intellectual vassalage to the formularies of the ruling establishment, no mandate to obey anything other than God's gift of reason could qualify one for 'humanity' in Christian England. *Some Thoughts Concerning Education* repudiated the Calvinist determinism of the Puritan past, making full humanity and salvation options of our own choosing.

5

A RENEWED CHRISTIAN POLITICS

Despite more than two decades of revisionist scholarship, Locke's political theory remains most often associated with the Western liberal constitutional state. His major statement on politics, the *Two Treatises of Government*, exercised significant influence during the eighteenth century, especially in Britain's American colonies where ideas of natural rights, popular sovereignty, contractual government, the legitimacy of revolution and of religious toleration together provided some of the intellectual background to the war for colonial independence.[1] Locke continues to be read as the defender of Whig principles, the key spokesperson for government exercising legislative, executive, and federative powers based upon known laws, not the will of men, for the autonomy of the individual and the moral propriety of property ownership. Thus to argue that his was a distinctly 'Christian' politics, particularly in light of the fact that the *Two Treatises* precludes the involvement of the magistrate in the religious affairs of his subjects, in effect transforming the state into an exclusively terrestrial organization, may seem peculiar. Even in light of the argument, initially made almost three decades ago, that one cannot fully appreciate Locke's politics without first coming to terms with his religious convictions and his reflections on community, one is still obliged to make explicit the precise connections between Locke's Christian faith and his anti-authoritarian formula for civil society.[2] It is necessary to show not only how resistance and revolution were justified whenever the magistrate violated the supreme law of nature, but also how such resistance was an essential requisite for salvation.

Locke's mature political philosophy addressed four problems which, according to James Tully, confronted every political thinker of the seventeenth century. The first, and most basic, concerned the nature of political power in light of the unsteady and often troublesome relations between magistrates and people as early modern nation states consolidated their status. The second involved the proper relationship of religion to politics, or the arrangement between church and state most likely to end the religious wars of the previous century. The third encompassed the actual practice of governing in an early modern mercantile setting, and the last problem centred on the types of knowledge appropriate to religion and political theory.[3] The recent scholarly work focusing on Locke's involvement in Exclusion Controversy politics and conspiracy as a backdrop to his political thought in *Two Treatises of Government* is certainly not misplaced, but it is nonetheless meaningful to recall that the issues facing the opponents of James, Duke of York, were not separate from wider European trends in government practice. One of the more immediate aims of the *Two Treatises* when it was composed in the early 1680s was to prevent England from becoming dominated by absolutist France. Civil wars inspired in no small part by theological disputes, religious persecution and government intolerance of inoffensive minorities, and the rise of the centralized and absolutist state, were all problems of immediate import to many of Locke's predecessors and contemporaries on the Continent. In fact this final issue, the growing power of bureaucratized and centralized states, had engaged the attention of theorists since monarchs had begun to undermine the traditional power of local elites throughout Western Europe around 1500.[4]

In the end, Locke's political philosophy contributed in an important way to what was nothing less than a fundamental shift in intellectual consciousness away from notions of duty and obligation toward one's superiors – the idea of the 'subject' who respectfully accepts his or her place in the great chain of being – and towards the standpoint of the pre-eminence of individual rights against traditional ruling elites – the idea of the 'citizen' for whom a humanly determined government is to provide specifically defined services. The relevance of this shift is difficult to overemphasize. In the England of Locke's youth, there were four categories of superiors who structured society and directed the lives of subjects: heads of households, magistrates, ecclesiastics, and God. Inferiors were thought to be incapable of self-direction, while superiors provided essential oversight and consistent moral guidance. Everyone in seventeenth-century England had a superior; children, servants, priests, even magistrates subordinated themselves to an immediate higher authority, with the monarch, situated at the top of the social apex, answering directly to God for his actions. It was thought that divine ordinance had established these hierarchies, and that each level was marked by a set of natural or acquired attributes appropriate to the wide variety of inferiors and superiors. The hierarchical pattern was thought to be prerequisite to unity and social stability, while all challenges to the age-old superiorities were associated with chaos and incoherence.[5]

Increasingly, throughout the next century and down into our own time, the claims of the individual to natural rights and equality in a political context would erode the centuries-old and almost instinctual acceptance of unchanging obligations in a hierarchically structured social order. Unlike the sixteenth-century reformer Martin Luther, whose endorsement of spiritual autonomy and the equality of souls before God did not extend to a concomitant equality in the political sphere, Locke's overall emphasis on the primacy of the individual's sovereignty in relations before his God transferred with *Two Treatises* to the dignity of the individual before the power of the previously omnicompetent confessional state. For Locke, political equality stemmed from natural equality at birth, where mankind was 'promiscuously born to all the same advantages of Nature, and the use of the same faculties' and where all were equals 'without Subordination or Subjection'. Locke could not discover 'any Manifest Declaration' of God's will establishing natural superiors under a system where adults were treated as children who would never possess the light of reason.[6] The Creator would never consent to absolutism because it required of mankind an abdication of their duty to preserve their individual freedom.

Securing that essential dignity and freedom meant, first and foremost, coming to terms with a tradition of absolutist thought which still held considerable sway in English intellectual circles, particularly within the Restoration Church of England. And English thought was by no means exceptional at this juncture. Indeed the notion that political power is derived immediately from God and entrusted with one person for the well-being of an otherwise factious people was commonplace across Western Europe; duty and submission formed the contours of existence for most of Europe's population. And defenders of non-resistance to absolute rulers were not reluctant to refer to chapter 13 of St Paul's letter to the Romans where the apostle claims that 'they, that resist, shall receive to themselves damnation' in order to affix eschatological penalties to all forms of dissent. References such as this one clearly assumed that the state was a Christian institution, and that the chief goal of the government was to advance the true faith and godly virtue. Monarchs may not have been free to act in an arbitrary manner under the absolutist paradigm, but their interpretation and application of the divine will was never to be contingent upon review by their subjects.

In addition, seventeenth-century social theory permitted fathers, as head of the family, a wide control over their wives and children. Power over children did not originate in consent, but in the mandate of God, the author of nature. And those who applied current social theory to politics insisted that the King derived his authority over his subjects from the same root. No allowance was made for the supposed rights of the subject because God had entrusted the monarch with the same paternal control over his subjects that Adam had enjoyed over his children. Sir Robert Filmer (1588–1653), who was much influenced in his thought by earlier opponents of the right to resistance, saw indivisible power and natural subjection as essential keys to public order, a view shared by a number of English authors – especially clergymen – throughout the seventeenth century, men who held that the privileges of Parliament were the exclusive gift of the King. Like Locke, Filmer believed that Scripture and reason were in harmony, but because reason was liable to error on political questions, one was on safer ground in turning to the inspired word for direction. And in Filmer's view the Book of Genesis clearly reveals that God had given the world to Adam, with his descendants inheriting his power following the well-established principle of primogeniture. Rulers answer to God alone for their actions, and especially for their sins.[7] We may not know who is the direct descendant of Adam, but this did not undermine the theory because God had empowered fathers to divide their title amongst their offspring. If the Fall of Adam had not taken place, then there would have been no need for the absolute power now held by kings. *Patriarcha* was probably composed before the Civil War, but it was not published until 1680 as Tory propaganda in the midst of the Exclusion Controversy; before the revolution of 1688–9 the text 'very nearly became the official state ideology'.[8] The very fact that Locke took Filmer seriously enough to write an exhaustive criticism of his interpretation of Scripture (the First Treatise), and the hard reality that Locke's argument in the Second Treatise was on the losing side of the struggle before 1688, is an important measure of just how influential the theory of patriarchal authority was in Restoration England.

Algernon Sydney and James Tyrrell, in addition to Locke, were joined by other Whigs during the Exclusion Crisis in detailing the

alleged errors contained in Filmer's theory. And in pamphlets support-
ing the revolution of 1688–9, attempts to discredit patriarchal theory
were commonplace. In Locke's case the author admitted in his preface
that the major part of the original manuscript of the First Treatise was
either lost or destroyed. What remained was a detailed rebuttal of
Filmer's scriptural exegesis in support of patriarchalism. The distor-
tions and inaccuracies are so overwhelming, according to Locke, that
'God must not be believed, though he speaks it himself, when he
says he does any thing, which will not consist with Sir Robert's
Hypothesis'.[9] Patriarchal theory could not be legitimized without first
distorting the plain words in Scripture. Perhaps more to the point,
Locke claimed that Scripture, in addressing early peoples in the
Old Testament, 'says not a word of their Rulers or forms of Government'. As early as 1660, in the *First Tract on Government*, Locke had
observed that 'Scripture speaks very little of politics anywhere' and it
appeared that 'God doth nowhere by distinct and particular prescriptions set down rules of governments and bounds to the magistrate's
authority'.[10]

In addition to challenging the veracity of Filmer's efforts to interpret
God's word, Locke adopted the effective rhetorical strategy of claiming
that his opponent's theory was innovative, without historical precedent. 'In this last age', Locke wrote, 'a generation of men has sprung
up among us, who would flatter princes with an Opinion, that they
have a Divine Right to absolute Power.' Locke sets himself the task of
exploding the novelty – and the injustice – of Filmer's theory so that
'Governments must be left again to the old way of being made by
contrivance, and the consent of Men making use of their reason to
unite together into Society.'[11] The old way referred to by Locke was
the tradition of European constitutionalism, for Locke a form of civil
government consistent with human reason, whereby political power is
the natural property of individuals delegated for specific ends, where
freedom and equality constitute the starting point in the creation of
institutional government. By the close of the century, absolutism
centred on the patriarchal model was no longer an instinctual and
therefore unquestioned body of doctrine. Indeed a growing restiveness
with political truths whose first order of business was to discourage
individual autonomy and personal responsibility coloured the general
intellectual climate during Locke's adult years. By the time he claimed
in *Two Treatises* that all men 'share in the same common Nature,
Faculties and Powers, are in Nature equal, and ought to partake in the
same common Rights and Privileges', what had once been instinctively

felt to be valid in politics was now shifting, and divine right doctrines like Filmer's, previously felt as facts, were giving rise to dissatisfaction and to suspicion of error.[12] Locke's theory cogently answered a deep-seated need to express duty in a new light, to feel a sense of control over one's own life while at the same time fulfilling a higher, indeed a divine mandate. No longer equivalent to blind submission and simple belief, duty now entailed a sustained personal inquiry on the part of each citizen and a judgement as to whether or not the natural law was being upheld by the magistrate. A restatement, a re-explanation was needed as the hierarchies of traditional political practice came under new scrutiny by men who could no longer accept absolutism on the grounds that a good God, especially one who had set as an important human purpose the pursuit and preservation of individual freedom, had willed such a system. As the old hierarchies in the heavens fell along with those of sublunary Roman Catholic ecclesiology, the stratified temporal order of politics was placed under greater scrutiny, pressed harder at every opportunity to legitimize itself before a public increasingly prone to scepticism.

Indeed in the midst of almost every discussion on politics during Locke's day was the potentially more troubling and divisive impact of sixteenth- and seventeenth-century epistemological scepticism. Doubts about the source, substance, and validity of all knowledge claims had really begun in earnest with the Reformation crisis of the early sixteenth century. Seeking to undercut the intellectual credentials of the Roman Catholic hierarchy, reformers who were engaged in this rule of faith controversy rebutted assertions of infallibility both with an appeal to Scripture and with an examination of human fallibility which excluded no one. In Locke's immediate context of composing the *Two Treatises* in the years 1679–83, Filmer's absolutist *Patriarcha* illustrated the arrogant and unproven epistemological premises of infallibilism with some precision, for the case in favour of divine right monarchy where subjects had no choice but to follow the dictates of the temporal head assumed that one knowledge base (the monarch's) was inherently superior to every other source. Locke sought to resolve a contemporary constitutional dispute and to prevent England from aligning itself with absolutist France by arguing that there was no evidence, scriptural or otherwise, that a single individual had been gifted with knowledge superior to another. And his proposed solution to the immediate problem facing the Shaftesbury circle was to find much broader application throughout Europe and America during the course of the eighteenth century and beyond.

Absolutist politics, it must be said, had nicely complemented a medieval world-view where human interests were centred on the eternal because government claimed to be of a piece with the larger divine plan. The central function of the state from the medieval period had been to advance and protect the true faith and to promote virtue within society – by coercion and force of arms if necessary. It was this position, critics attested, which had played no small part in protracting the European wars of religion in the century after the Reformation, as secular rulers first asserted control over their national churches and then harnessed the ideological fervour of religious differences to more traditional quarrels over territory, with the inevitable result being the destruction of property and loss of life for Europe's innocents. Locke too could claim the mantle of medieval priorities with a political theory designed to better enforce the law of nature or the divine mandate for humankind, but he did so in a manner which both denied government its traditional competence over religious affairs and, even more crucially, its claim to divine origin. With *Two Treatises* the purpose of the state was to preserve life and property, not religion. But the temporal order was still firmly subordinated to the spiritual one, notwithstanding the author's claims regarding the sanctity of property and the government's paramount duty to protect it, because government founded through human consensus was to provide the conditions under which each individual might best pursue his search for lasting happiness. Despite what Locke took to be the human origins of civil society, despite the fact that government is not charged with the inculcation of Christian doctrine, Locke's was a God-conscious politics where eternal laws formed the cornerstone of human action, and where civil society was the arena within which those laws found their most consistent enforcement. People should obey the law of nature because all are 'the workmanship of one omnipotent, and infinitely wise maker; all the servants of one sovereign master, sent into the world by his order, and about his business'. We are God's creation, He is our natural superior, and we have no right to destroy ourselves or to place our lives under the discretionary control of an absolute ruler. To do so would be tantamount to denying God his proprietary rights. All laws drawn up by the legislative branch in civil society, therefore, must 'be conformable to the Law of Nature, i.e. to the Will of God'.[13] No other formulation of the place of legislation in the affairs of men was possible if society was to conform to God's larger purposes.

Locke's first reflections on politics, the *Two Tracts on Government*, shares some presuppositions with his later thought, but overall there is little in the political theory of the early Locke to identify him with the concepts closely associated with his later reputation. *Two Tracts*, as we have seen, was composed in the immediate aftermath of 20 years of conflict where varying attempts to impose appropriate standards of religious practice had resulted in unprecedented political turmoil. Religion served as 'a perpetual foundation of war and contention: all those flames that have made such havoc and desolation in Europe, and have not been quenched but with the blood of so many millions, have been at first kindled with coals from the altar'.[14] Peace and order being the paramount concerns of many like Locke in the early 1660s, the Oxford tutor drew a sharp distinction between religious belief and religious practice. The former, being the genuine and essential part of faith, was a private affair and should be left unhindered by the civil authority. Prescribed forms of worship, on the other hand, were matters of indifference to God, and in the interest of public safety and the good ordering of society it must be the magistrate's prerogative to set the standards. It would, of course, be ideal if all men could pursue their own form of worship in peace, but the record of Levellers, Diggers, and Republicans since the 1640s made such a laudable option impractical. The early *Two Tracts on Government* offered a very bleak view of the behaviour of the majority of Englishmen, and since for Locke at this stage inward belief and public action were separate spheres, obedience even to the dictates of a corrupt and sinful magistrate was mandatory.[15] He drew no distinction between the legislative and executive branches of government in this work, and while the authority of the law of nature was assumed, Locke made no effort to clarify the epistemological foundations of our knowledge of the law's content.

Given the authoritarian character of these early writings, the transformation in Locke's thinking by the end of the decade of the 1660s is extraordinary. The unpublished 'Essay Concerning Toleration', composed after the start of his friendship with Shaftesbury and with the hope that Charles II might grant an indulgence to Dissenters, reversed his earlier conviction that an absolute magistrate was in a privileged position to determine appropriate forms of religious practice. More importantly, Locke for the first time linked inward belief and conscience with outward behaviour or action, including one's manner of public worship. Both now became central to the search for salvation, and in this most important business in life no person could presume to take responsibility for another by setting arbitrary standards of doctrine and worship. As the memory of Interregnum politics faded, as the persecution of Dissenters intensified, and as fear (misplaced or not) of popery and Stuart authoritarianism increased amongst Shaftesbury's associates, Locke concluded that the magistrate was ill-equipped to meddle in affairs involving the salvation of souls. The Clarendon Code was doing little to advance the aims of civil harmony and national prosperity during the 1660s, and while thousands of nonconformists were impoverished, jailed and transported, their ranks continued to hold firm to their version of the truth. The author of the 'Essay Concerning Toleration', while not denying that the magistrate had a duty to regulate religious practice in the interests of peace, recommended that toleration of dissent could indeed further the overall national good. Compulsory uniformity, he was convinced, ignited civil unrest, and Anglican clergymen were wrong to insist that uniformity was merely a response to unrest.

Locke's reflections on politics before he entered Shaftesbury's service took for granted the existence of civil society without exploring its origins. Institutional government was accepted as a perennial necessity of men who were inclined to highlight and exploit differences at every available opportunity. By 1673, when the King's heir, the Catholic James, Duke of York, married the Catholic princess Mary of Modena, Whig fears of a French-style absolutism being erected in England informed much of the debate about the fate of mixed monarchy and the ancient constitution. Louis XIV's subsidies to the Stuart royal family, together with his persecution of French Protestants, combined with parliamentary complaints of corruption in the judiciary and suspicions that the Crown sought the creation of a standing army, issued in the formation of a Whig interest intent on arresting the dangerous trends. Andrew Marvell's *Account of the Growth of Popery and Arbitrary Government* (1677) captured the essence of the Whig position when he declared that 'There has now for divers years, a design been carried on, to change the lawful government of England into an absolute tyranny.'[16] By 1679 the focal point of the effort to reverse this trend was the parliamentary attempt to alter the succession. During and immediately after the parliamentary efforts to exclude James, Duke of York, Locke revisited the entire question of the roots of civil society and political obligation, finding in his search no grounds for the popular and persuasive patriarchal theories of staunch royalists and Church of England clerics.

Locke was aware not only of Filmer's apologia but of a broader, and more influential, Church of England defence of absolutism which had been communicated on a regular basis in parish churches throughout the country since 1600. Locke even stated in the preface to the First Treatise that the deceased Filmer would not be worth rebutting 'had not the Pulpit, of late Years, publickly owned his Doctrine, and made it the Current Divinity of the Times'.[17] The doctrine of absolute sovereignty enjoyed the support of a number of political theorists who were also Anglican clergymen, and all of whom were eager to maintain the Church's monopoly of political power established under the Act of Uniformity of 1662 and in the face both of recurrent calls for a toleration and the King's own intermittent preference for a more broad-based Church of England. Locke understood that religious persecution more often than not accompanied the establishment of a tyrannical government, and while there is a distinctly secular tone to the Second Treatise, the author was very much concerned to defend the rights of religious minorities. The High Church bishops of the period 1660–85 were determined to strengthen the claims of the Crown in their own efforts to restore the Church's title to be the final arbiter in matters of faith and morals. Locke believed that both the Crown and the Established Church, and most directly the latter, had to be confronted if the evils of absolutism, its potential for stripping subjects of their fundamental duty to establish their own relationship with God, were to be avoided. In *A Letter Concerning Toleration*, issued just before the appearance of *Two Treatises*, Locke took direct aim at the Established Church and its patriarchal apologists when he stated that true religion 'is not instituted in order to the erecting an external pomp, nor to the exercising of compulsory force; but to the regulating of men's lives according to the rules of virtue and piety' through love and persuasion exclusively.[18] Attacking High Church apologists for the Stuart Crown, men whom Locke believed were primarily interested in enhancing their own access to political power and dominion, was an essential part of the strategy for basing politics on a natural law foundation. Removing the influence of clerical elites from government through the adoption of a toleration would also effectively put an end to the religious conflicts and civil wars which had become the distressing hallmark of European life.

The *Letter Concerning Toleration* did much more than repeat the sentiments first expressed in the unpublished 'Essay on Toleration' of 1667. In fact the central appeal of the *Letter* is to the subordinate nature of political life and to the circumscribed character of priestly and magisterial authority for the simple reason that salvation must be our pre-eminent and perpetual concern.[19] The individual who is not tolerant of others, who does not manifest his Christian character through holiness of life, purity of manners, and meekness of spirit 'appears careless about his own salvation', while anyone who accepts the religion of the magistrate without an inward persuasion of mind that all it teaches and prescribes is true, precludes any hope for eternal reward. 'The care of the Salvation of Mens Souls cannot belong to the Magistrate; because, though the rigour of Laws and the force of Penalties were capable to convince and change Mens minds, yet would not that help at all to the Salvation of their Souls.' No member of a Church can be a sincere and willing participant in public worship unless he or she is bound to that particular communion by 'the certain expectation of eternal Life. A Church then is a Society of Members voluntarily uniting to this end.' In a powerful illustration of the practical limits of temporal power, Locke reminds his readers that if the prince should order him to follow a mercantile career, he would not hesitate to comply because should he fail to prosper, the prince would have the power to reverse his fortunes. Such, however, was not the case with respect to religion, for if the official and compulsory religion should turn out to be false, 'What security can be given for the Kingdom of Heaven'?[20]

More than 35 years ago Peter Laslett firmly established that *Two Treatises* was not written as an intellectual defence of the Revolution of 1688–9, as had been assumed by generations of readers, but instead was composed much earlier, during the Exclusion Crisis between 1679 and 1681, as a rebuttal to the absolutist arguments set forth in Filmer's *Patriarcha*. In 1986 Richard Ashcraft produced a forceful challenge to this dating, arguing instead that both the First and the Second Treatises were composed only after the dissolution of the 1681 Oxford Parliament, when the constitutional option to preventing the succession of James, Duke of York, appeared closed. In other words, according to Ashcraft the work which was published in 1690 as *Two Treatises* was written to legitimize armed resistance after the failure of the Exclusion Parliaments. Shaftesbury and other Whig leaders, Locke included, are said to have attended meetings of conspirators against the Crown, and the Second Treatise to have been written in the wake of these meetings. Additionally, Ashcraft argues that the radical nature of the Second Treatise's defence of individual rights was designed to appeal to lower social groups, artisans, tradesmen and workmen, who would be more sympathetic to revolution than the aristocrats and gentry who had failed to secure Exclusion by legal means. Locke's call for revolution, then, would have involved a much wider cross-section of the social hierarchy than that which eventually engaged in the successful 1688–9 affair. Despite Locke's rather conservative reflections on property in the Second Treatise, the work as a whole was tailored to win the support of nonconformists, artisans, and common working men who were now declared inherently rational.[21]

More recently John Marshall and David Wootton, while agreeing with much of Ashcraft's argument, have made some important clarifications to the story. Wootton dates the composition of the Second Treatise to late 1681, while Marshall provides evidence to set the earliest time of composition of the First Treatise to 1681 and the Second Treatise to late 1682 or even early 1683. This later date was after King Charles began *quo warranto* proceedings against the charter of the corporation of London, the result of which was to give the Crown control of the franchise in the city and to supervise the sheriffs who appointed London juries. Both actions seriously compromised Whig power in the capital. It was, after all, a Whig-dominated jury which acquitted Shaftesbury of treason in November 1681, after the King had decided to pursue a vindictive policy against supporters of Exclusion. Awareness that Charles II was poised to alter the franchise and influence jury selection at a time when Parliament was not in session only strengthened the suspicions – and the fears – of those who saw absolutism as the long-range goal of the Stuart Crown, and who advocated armed resistance in order to preclude that disaster.[22]

In addition, Marshall takes issue with Ashcraft's assumption that Locke intended the Second Treatise to appeal to men from lower social orders by stressing the importance of an individual right to resistance. The conservative nature of Locke's preference for the existing constitutional structure, together with his concern to maintain existing property rights and his unwillingness to sanction resistance whenever individuals – even a majority – sought to secure a more virtuous, equalitarian, or progressive society, appears to support Marshall's claim that Locke was aiming to attract the backing of the gentry, yeoman and merchants who had supported Exclusion and who now faced the prospect of royal absolutism. In the Second Treatise political society is not dissolved whenever the people elect to adopt another form of political organization. Only when the existing government dissolves itself by failing to fulfil its expressly stated minimal obligations can resistance, the appeal to heaven, be justified. And only a clear and deliberate pattern on the part of the government, a design to take property and to abrogate the legal process which ensures personal liberties, qualifies for Locke as legitimate grounds for action against

the magistrate. Only then is the trust that people had originally placed
in government irrevocably broken because absolutism seeks to take
from men something which they cannot surrender: each man is the
property of God and we have no power to alienate that which we do
not own. Resistance to tyranny, to the sinfulness at the root of
absolutism, is the defence of God's property. The abusive monarch
'divests himself of his Crown and Dignity, and returns to the state of a
private Man, and the people become free and superior' whenever he
attempts to alienate his subjects' freedom.[23]

In works written around the time of this manuscript by men who,
like Locke, were involved in discussions about possible resistance in
1682, and who accepted that governments were created by consent,
both Robert Ferguson and Algernon Sydney offered views on the
purpose of government far removed from Locke's more modest
demands. Ferguson's *Impartial Enquiry into the Administration of Affairs
in England* (1684) declared that all political authority issued directly
from God, while Sydney's *Discourses Upon Government*, probably written
between 1681 and 1683, condoned the notion that a government
might be overturned if the people decided that another might better
advance their temporal interests. For Locke all governments were
consensual, man-made institutions whose instrumental and minimalist
task was sharply delineated. While not issuing directly from God in a
divinely appointed fashion, civil society was to ensure that men had
the opportunity to pursue their quest for eternal reward unhindered by
any state-supported clerical establishment. The protection of property
– lives, liberties, and estates – provided the essential environment of
security under which people might pursue their greatest happiness.
Locke did not call for a different form of government in the Second
Treatise, rather he argued that a change of personnel was needed if the
balanced constitution which had been so successful in defending
property in the past were to be restored and stabilized. The true rebel
in 1682 was Charles II, a man who was forcing his people into
resistance because he had not called Parliament when it was needed
and a man who was using his prerogative powers in a deliberate
attempt to rule without consent. Resistance, Locke maintained in a
major conceptual innovation, was possible without upsetting the
existing social structure and, just as importantly, without threatening
existing property relationships. As Marshall points out, it was this type
of argument that was most likely to win the support of gentry with
clear (and unpleasant) memories of radical calls for fundamental social
and economic change during the Commonwealth period.

When the revolution did come in 1688–9, Locke published his manuscript with few revisions because he felt that it faithfully represented the limited nature of the changes realized after the flight of James II. Unfortunately, few of the Whig leaders were willing to endorse even this conservative interpretation of the dissolution of James II's government. Even his friend James Tyrrell demurred at Locke's contention that political power reverts to the people, arguing instead that executive power returns to representative bodies or great councils.[24] Adopting instead the strained notion of an abdication, the members of the Convention Parliament were unwilling to accept the potentially explosive notion that government had been reconstructed anew by the people after James had violated his trust by his sustained efforts to imitate Louis XIV. Locke may have endorsed mixed monarchy and a restrictive franchise; he may, as he stated in the preface, have merely desired to make William's title to the throne unimpeachable, but his theoretical defence of the right to resistance under extremely restricted circumstances, involving as it did the idea of natural freedom together with the right of individual armed resistance, was not the sort of defence of the ancient constitution favoured by the majority of politicians in 1689.[25]

Locke had begun the Second Treatise not with an historical or legalistic inquiry into the form of the supposed ancient constitution, a method preferred by most commentators, but rather by outlining a state of nature or natural state of mankind where human equality and perfect freedom informed the subsequent creation of a civil order wholly incompatible with the authoritarian direction of his earlier thought. In the state of nature, which for Locke appears to have been a historical reality and not simply a logical fiction, political power belonged naturally to self-governing individuals who were aware of their divinely appointed equality.[26] All having equal jurisdiction, men were free 'to order their actions, and dispose of their possessions and persons, as they think fit, within the bounds of the law of nature'.[27] In addition, each individual was empowered to execute the law of nature – to judge and to punish – if and when another member violated any of its provisions. Hobbes had insisted that outside of civil society individuals are left without any formal rule to guide them and thus there could be no moral rule applicable to human action. The author of Leviathan indicated that in the state of nature there is no justice or injustice, no eternal right or wrong.[28] Locke disagreed with this radical position, asserting that there is a known positive natural law, accessed through mature reason. Locke declined to 'enter into the particulars of the law of nature' in the Second Treatise, saying at one point that it is 'unwritten, and so no where to be found but in the minds of Men', but he does urge that there is such a law and that it is as 'intelligible and plain' as the positive laws of commonwealths. In this he was following a well-accepted tradition upheld by such writers as Grotius and Pufendorf. It is this internal law, discovered through the use of reason, that 'teaches all mankind, who will but consult it, that being all equal and independent, no one ought to harm another in his life, health, liberty, or possessions'. There is also a basic equality in the state of nature, and this equality is not surrendered at the point of entry into civil society. He claimed the authority of 'the judicious Hooker' for the view that men are equal by nature, knowing that it was an extremely controversial and innovative notion in a century where patriarchal theory exercised great influence, and where natural superiors were to be found at every turn.[29] Locke also claimed Hooker's authority to rebut those who would question whether any men ever actually subsisted in a state of nature.

The principal reason for leaving the state of nature and entering into civil society, however, arises from the fact that there are always transgressors of the law of nature, including those who will not exercise restraint when punishing violations of the common standard. Indeed while the ideal picture of the state of nature is 'a state of peace, good will, mutual assistance and preservation', human partiality created a situation where each person was 'constantly exposed to the invasion of others' and where life itself became 'full of fears and continual dangers'.[30] The major source of these disputes in a state of nature marked by economic development and the introduction of money stemmed from differences over property –'quarreling about title' or 'about the largeness of possession'. Locke did not insist, like Hobbes, that the conditions in the state of nature were akin to perpetual warfare, but he did conclude that peaceful coexistence would be extremely difficult to maintain in a situation where every man was empowered to enforce the law of nature on his fellows. In effect Locke was again acknowledging that while theoretically mankind was capable of freely obeying the law of reason or nature, in practice the expectation had never been realized. Human egotism and the unwillingness to follow the golden rule made civil society and an independent arbiter essential.

In making the decisive transition from a state of nature to civil society, then, the sole objective was to escape the condition where the majority of men were no great respecters of justice, where persons were prone to violate the rule of reason, which is the rule of law in a state of nature. For Locke, individuals in the state of nature agree, conditionally, to transfer the right to judge disputes to a common legislature and judiciary, while the right to execute the law is given to a common executive. Thus the political state, contrary to patriarchal theory, is not a natural condition, but a voluntary one, always circumscribed in extent. In defining political power as 'a Right of making Laws with Penalties of Death, and consequently all less Penalties, for the Regulating and Preserving of Property, and of employing the force of the Community, in the Execution of such Laws, and in defence of the Common-wealth from Foreign Injury', Locke was addressing what he took to be the three essential features of government. Legislative power to regulate lives, activities and possessions, executive power to enforce agreed laws, and federative power to wage war in order to protect the community, all emerge out of the shared need to establish an impartial application of the laws of nature. While political society is made up of representative governing institutions, original political power remains with the people, and they retain the right to resume that power should it be wielded in a tyrannical manner, whether by the legislature or executive. And tyranny was introduced whenever 'the Governour, however intitled, makes not the Law, but his Will, the Rule', whenever the good of the community is subordinated to the magistrate's arbitrary demands and appetite, or, alternatively, to the demands of manipulative religious elites who have won the ear of the magistrate.[31] The authority of government, then, originates in the authentic powers of equal individuals in the state of nature who establish an agreed-upon convention for civil society. Locke's objective was to persuade his audience, the majority of whom had been raised to believe in the natural subjection of Christian men and women to existing political rulers, of the need for a new basis of Christian obligation, one where the gift of reason was exercised as intended by the Creator. Under this new model, reason or the law of nature, which had earlier served as the standard to settle disputes in the state of nature, now became the benchmark for all legislation and all executive action in civil society, and in the final analysis as the axiom by which citizens judged their government.

When Locke defined political power as 'a Right of making Laws with Penalties of Death, and consequently all less Penalties, for the Regulating and Preserving of Property' he was using the word property rather broadly to include life, personal liberty, and material possessions or estate.[32] No one had the inherent right to alienate his own life, thus it would be illegitimate to award government absolute control over our person. And material possessions, property in the narrow sense, since they proceed from mixing our labour with the soil, an undertaking which antedates the formation of civil society, cannot be arbitrarily taken from us without violating a law of nature and, in civil society, without dissolving the contract. Locke's theory of property at one level appears to place the premium upon egoistic, individual rights to the land and its products at the expense of the potential good of the community. At the very least his theory seemed to clash with an earlier view of property where ownership entailed restrictions on the owner, social controls which dictated the terms of customary land tenure and usage; at most it amounted to a moral basis for laissez-faire capitalism.[33] Locke, however, needed to address Filmer's contention that property, like political power, belonged entirely to the prince. Indeed English law prior to 1660 accepted the feudal principle that the possession and use of land derived from the monarch. Thomas Hobbes had asserted that government is an essential prerequisite to property, 'no Mine and Thine' being possible without a sovereign to police the convention.[34] If, as Locke contended, property originated with labour in the state of nature, by men tilling the soil and producing enough to provide for their immediate subsistence, then it would be untenable to allow the King control over the product of another man's toil. Man was God's special creation and was designed by God to labour and improve the products of the earth as part of a larger natural law requirement to enhance the quality of existence for all. 'I think that it will be but a very modest Computation to say, that of the Products of the Earth useful to the Life of Man nine tenths are the effects of labour.'[35] It was obvious that unimproved nature could not provide for anything but the barest of human necessities. In addition, Locke was convinced that the protection of property was essential to the maintenance of our God-given personal freedom because it enabled the possessor to escape any form of servitude to another.

If, with the introduction of money by common consent in the state of nature, some men acquired more land and wealth through their own inventiveness and industriousness, then Locke was convinced that the resulting economic inequalities were in large measure legitimate. The rational and enterprising were now entitled to sell their surplus for a profit; the subsequent growth of property differentials and the rise of commercial activity was in no sense anti-Christian, for those who exchanged the produce of their land did nothing to counter God's design that the earth be improved for the benefit of all. Whatever reservations he may have entertained about the effects of money on the potential scale of ownership, Locke was satisfied that the introduction of a cash economy had facilitated the advancement of Europe's, and in particular England's, well-being over all other parts of the globe. This position would doubtless have appealed to the gentry and merchant elements of the population who composed Locke's primary audience and whose livelihoods were linked to expanding markets and the ever-increasing consumption of goods. Neal Wood has argued forcefully, and convincingly, that Locke was no democrat. Men should be permitted to improve themselves regardless of birth or rank because self-help and application were laudable qualities in any Christian, but Locke nevertheless 'accepted the existing structure of society charac-terized by a hierarchy of class and status and a system of wide property differentials' on the assumption that these differences were largely the result of industriousness and personal acumen.[36] Producers were believers who acted upon God's call for every person to embrace the ethic of hard work.

Still he was undoubtedly troubled by the increasing tendency on the part of men to seek more than they needed after the introduction of money. The acceptance of money occasioned the exacerbation of human sinfulness; need and convenience were replaced by greed and covetousness, and the disputes over property which it fostered were powerful – and distressing – motives leading to the creation of civil society.[37] According to Locke, God specifically conveyed to each individual in the state of nature a right 'to the use of those things, which were serviceable for his Subsistence'. Any subsequent develop-ment of property relations, whether in the state of nature or in civil society, still presupposed this basic right to subsistence, even if property for exclusive individual use was agreed by everyone.[38] Locke thus clearly defended everyone's natural right to subsistence, even in the wake of a money economy and the subsequent massive inequalities of wealth which it endorsed. It was on these grounds, for example, that he challenged the legitimacy of primogeniture, a system designed to deny all but the eldest male use of the parent's property. When Locke was appointed a member of the Board of Trade in 1696, he reiterated this position in a memorandum on Poor Law reform. Every human being, he insisted, had a right to food, drink, and clothing, and the common good of society demanded criminal sanctions against any poor relief administrator who failed to meet this basic obligation of the law of nature.[39]

Locke's view of social relations may have permitted the holding of unequal amounts of property through industry or inheritance, and he also may have accepted that the wages received by labourers did not have to be equal to the value that they had added to the products of nature, but he did not believe that his affirmation of existing property relations in late seventeenth-century England would be morally justifiable if it led to a situation where any inhabitant was thereby effectively denied a means of subsistence. Locke's many disparaging references to the propertyless labourers aside, to deny the 'vulgar', the 'untamd beast', the 'rabble' basic subsistence was to seek to destroy an innocent being whose fate belonged in the hands of God alone. Secondarily it would also make more likely the very conditions of social instability most conducive to violent revolution from below. In other words, Locke did not endorse the right to unlimited capitalist accumulation on behalf of the ruling class without respect for its impact on propertyless men.[40] Ownership of property, no matter how extensive or how limited, continued to involve social obligations, natural law theory continued to direct action. As the Sixth Commandment enjoined us to preserve our neighbour as ourself, so the Second Table of the Decalogue prohibited self-advancement without social responsibility. Men continued to have moral claims on one another, and no conventions respecting political organization could change this fact.

In the introduction to the *Essay* he had observed that God has given man 'Whatsoever is necessary for the Conveniences of Life, and Information of Vertue; and has put within the reach of their Discovery the comfortable Provision for this Life, and the way that leads to a better.' His view on the origin, accumulation, and use of property was designed to provide conditions under which God's workmanship would be preserved, the quality of their terrestrial existence improved so that more effort might be exerted on the moral duties essential to salvation. Unlimited acquisitiveness is not the end of labour and property, not, at least, for the heaven-directed man. In the education of children the skilful tutor must 'teach them to part with what they have easily and freely to their Friends'; covetousness must be rooted out 'and the contrary Quality of a Readiness to impart to others, implanted'.[41] For those who had been successful in property and trade, for the industrious gentleman who had enhanced the common store through better land management and overall business skill, social obligations and expectations only increased; the deference, obedience, and acceptance of the existing social order on the part of the working poor had to be earned by society's natural leaders. The beneficial features of a market society could only be justified if all members of that society, rich and poor, continued to observe the law of nature which directs us 'to preserve the rest of Mankind'.[42] Government might have been instituted on the rather mundane and self-interested grounds of better protecting property, but property, like everything else in this state of mediocrity, was to be viewed as a trust, held briefly while we are alive and in the knowledge that its use and improvement were to provide greater benefit to all.

There are two final, and quite disturbing, issues that cloud the entire foregoing discussion, and they have troubled almost every modern scholar of Locke's political thought. The first concerns the impact of Locke's ideas regarding political society and property on the Amerindian population of North America, how the dispossession of the Amerindian was legitimized by the overwhelming power of Locke's theory of popular sovereignty. The second and equally important issue concerns the status of African-American slaves in England's new world colonial empire.

We know from his final library collection that Locke was familiar with the lifestyles of aboriginal peoples, especially those living in North America. He read accounts of travellers and explorers, and his work for the government during the 1690s involved him in a number of policy-making decisions concerning the colonial system.[43] He described America in his *Two Treatises* as an example of the state of nature and also associated it with the earliest point in historical development. When the Europeans came into contact with the aborigines, they interacted in this state of nature, and conflicts were often described by European settlers as 'just wars' against a people who in some manner or another had violated natural law precepts.[44] From the earliest point of English settlement in North America, colonists had taken the position that Amerindian political organization was illegitimate and that the aborigines' failure to settle and improve the land stripped them of any claim to proprietorship over it. The hunting and gathering culture of the Amerindians meant for the seventeenth-century English settlers that the land was vacant, unimproved, and therefore open for European-style labour-based development.

Locke confirmed this overall picture when he asserted that the Amerindians, lacking a formal legal system, a legislature or a regular executive, could not claim proper statehood. In like fashion Locke did not recognize the collectivist notions of land ownership embraced by

networks of kinship and custom in Amerindian culture. Because people
living in the state of nature had not mixed their labour to improve the
land, because they had not taken the first steps towards a system of
market agriculture, settlers were fully justified in inaugurating their
familiar European system of labour-based property relationships
where God's bounty was improved for the benefit of all. As Locke
stated unequivocally in the Second Treatise, God may have given the
world to mankind in common in a state of nature, but he did not
intend that they should leave it 'common and uncultivated' as the
underproducing Amerindians preferred. Rather the earth was given to
'the use of the Industrious and Rational, (and Labour was his Title to
it)'.[45] The Amerindians' non-sedentary labour, the organization and
skill involved in hunting, fishing, and gathering, did not qualify as
industriousness, while their limited interest in the accumulation of
earthly possessions together with their pre-monetary economy suggested something less than compliance with the divine mandate.
Devoid of the ethic of improvement and living in a state of nature,
the estimate of Amerindian culture contained in *Two Treatises* provided encouragement to the dynamic and ultimately exploitative
nature of English colonialism during Locke's lifetime and beyond.

When we turn to Locke's position on slavery, the difficulties multiply. Given Locke's oft-repeated assertions regarding the fundamental
equality of human beings and the natural rights which all enjoy as
creatures fashioned by a benevolent deity, how do we explain his
considerable financial and administrative involvement in African
slavery and the international slave trade? What relationship exists
between his theory of slavery resulting from captives taken in a 'just
war', discussed in the Second Treatise, and Locke's very personal
involvement in the systematic denial of natural rights to Black Africans
in the American colonies?

In addition to his investing £600 in the Royal African Company in
1672, a company which enjoyed a monopoly in the slave trade, Locke
also invested with the Company of Merchant Adventurers to trade
with the Bahamas, organized to stimulate planting and trade through
the use of slaves in that recently acquired English colony. Locke also
worked as secretary to the Lords Proprietors of Carolina during
1668–75, an assignment that involved him in the task of drawing
up, under Shaftesbury's supervision and perhaps as a co-author, the
1669 *Fundamental Constitutions of Carolina*. There it was confirmed that
'Every freeman of Carolina shall have absolute power and authority
over his negro slaves, of what opinion or religion soever.'[46] Much later,

in 1696, when he was appointed a commissioner of the Board of Trade, Locke was involved in drafting a number of dispatches to various governors in the royal colonies, and the treatment of slaves and the operation of the slave trade were often discussed.

In the *Fundamental Constitutions* slaves were to be allowed to become members of the church of their choosing. And in a set of instructions sent from the Board of Trade to Governor Francis Nicholson of Virginia in 1698, Locke advised the passing of a law to provide the death penalty for anyone convicted of 'the willful killing of Indians and Negroes'. In addition the governor was encouraged to facilitate the conversion of 'Negroes and Indians' to Christianity. But slaves who were Christians and who presumably as Christians were to be afforded the liberty of conscience advocated in *A Letter Concerning Toleration* were not afforded the right to gainsay the system which kept them in physical bondage. *A Letter* had stressed that when the magistrate's conception of the public good clashed with the viewpoint of Christian subjects, God alone would judge between the parties. Slaves may have been Christians, but in the world of natural superiors which Locke had worked to overturn, Black Africans occupied a status unequal to citizenship. Even the acknowledgement that Africans possessed immortal souls did not improve their material conditions, for 'religion ought to alter nothing in any man's civil estate'.[47] If Locke was the sole author of this passage in the *Fundamental Constitutions*, it would seem to be consistent with his paraphrase on one of St Paul's Epistles that he wrote toward the end of his life. Paraphrasing 1 Corinthians 7:24, Locke said that 'In whatsoever state a man is called in the same he is to remain notwithstanding any privileges of the gospel', a passage likely to confirm his earlier distinction between religious and civil freedom.

In the Second Treatise Locke had allowed for the institution of slavery only when those in bondage were 'Captives taken in a just War', a conflict undertaken by innocents against an unjust aggressor. The victory of the just entitles them to punish the aggressor with death, but they may choose to delay the sentence and make use of the person who has quitted reason in attempting to deny others their rights and freedoms. Locke made no effort to link African-African chattel slaves with captives taken in any such just war, and his silence on the roots of contemporary slave-holding practice makes it difficult to explain the contradiction between natural rights theory and the *de facto* slavery in the English colonies, a system which Locke both participated in and benefited from.[48] John Dunn once called Locke's silence 'immoral evasion' and this view has been endorsed by more recent students.[49] Unwilling to deny slaves their basic humanity by precluding their access to baptism and Christian communion, opposed to the unprovoked violence against slaves that he knew was a constant problem in the colonies, Locke nevertheless failed to explain the disjunction between his theory and his practice. In this he would be followed by many others in succeeding generations, strengthening an institution at odds with the fundamental tenets of the Christian story.

In the eighteenth century David Hume, who had boldly removed God and divine intentions from all discussion of political authority and legislation, criticized Locke's model polity in *Two Treatises* for being synonymous with the traditional political institutions of early modern England; Locke's ideal government, in other words, was still composed of King in Parliament, provided of course that one had the right type of King.[50] And indeed Locke was convinced that the English constitutional arrangement was best adapted to the promotion of individual freedom and self-reliance outside and above one's traditional associations in guild, church, family and local community. Free and reasonable men had been placed by their author at a particular point in the Great Chain of creation. At the apex of sentient creation but at the humbler reaches of intellectual life, the great designer had called upon man to follow reason in his social relationships, to preserve himself and to multiply, to improve the common store, although God had not prescribed the exact details of the political structure requisite to the charge. But with the law of nature serving as the fixed rule by which God had fashioned and now governed the universe, reasonable men might work out the particulars of civil order where the inherent dignity of the person was maintained and the material conditions by which they lived their lives were enriched.

Like the rest of creation, God had set humankind a purpose, a telos, and it was not limited to this world. Government was merely instrumental, a convention built by human minds for limited purposes. It could not deny man the use of reason – a gift from God – nor could it impel him to be good – an obligation to God. It could not prescribe a particular form of worship, nor could it impose bodily sanctions on those whose chosen path to the divine verged from the one travelled by the prince. For this prince, and here was the heart of the matter, was merely a human being whose God-given nature differed in no fundamental respect from his subjects. Authority and superiority continued to exist in the Lockean state, but it was an agreed hierarchy, not a divinely commissioned one, static and unimpeachable. The logic of Luther's 'priesthood of all believers', alone before God and without natural spiritual directors, had been expanded to a sphere of inferior value, but a sphere nevertheless preliminary to the rewards of the greater. To recognize how far modern Western political culture has moved away from Locke's God-directed politics is to come to terms with what is perhaps the most fundamental relocation in political thought over the last 300 years.

6

AN ENLIGHTENMENT LEGACY

It should not surprise us to learn that Locke spent the last morning before his death on the afternoon of 28 October 1704 listening to Damaris Masham read the Psalms, or that the night before the entire Masham family had met in his room for evening prayers. He was said to have reminded those present that the continued practice of their duties, together with a regular and attentive reading of Holy Scriptures, would bring them happiness in this world and 'possession of eternal felicity in the other'. In one of his last letters written before his death, Locke told the Deist Anthony Collins that the vanity of this life was only compensated by 'the consciousness of doeing well and in the hopes of an other life'. Locke composed an epitaph for his gravestone which stated that his virtues, if any, were too slight to serve as an example to others; at any rate, the best examples were to be found in the Gospels.[1] He was buried, following the instructions in his will, in the churchyard of High Laver, Essex, near the Masham home at Oates. He requested an unadorned wooden coffin and a small private ceremony, and both of these entreaties were, to the best of our knowledge, honoured by his nephew and closest living relative, Peter King.

Locke's death in the fourth year of the century of Enlightenment, the century of the *philosophes* and the age of revolution in France and America, signalled the close of responses to his ideas formulated within the context of problems peculiar to late seventeenth-century England, and the beginning of interpretations set within new social, religious, and political situations. Locke's eighteenth century legacy, in other words, was shaped by his heirs to fit the problems unique to a variety of historical circumstances. Thus it would be misleading to speak of the early eighteenth century as a period 'when Locke reigned virtually unchallenged'.[2] Whatever Locke's intentions may have been, his work was moulded by succeeding generations in order to address new difficulties in fresh settings. The legacy was unquestionably diffuse, but often the application of Lockean solutions to later problems had little relationship to the original contextual intentions of the author. And nowhere is this transformation more dramatic than in the eighteenth century's disregard for Locke's religious sensibility, his lifelong concern to fit the entirety of the human experience into a larger theological framework of meaning and purpose.

When, in the *Conduct of the Understanding*, Locke observed that theology remained the one science 'incomparably above all the rest' because it involved 'the Comprehension of all other Knowledge directed to its true End; i.e. the Honour and Veneration of the Creator, and the Happiness of Mankind', he was simply repeating what had by this juncture become a commonplace in his thought. The study of theology, independent of secular interests, was every man's duty, at least those who owned the title 'reasonable'. 'This is that Science which would truly enlarge Men's Minds, were it study'd, or permitted to be study'd every where, with that Freedom, Love of Truth and Charity which it teaches.'[3] The *Essay Concerning Human Understanding* had set narrow limits to man's knowledge of the world after a rigorous empirical approach to the operations of the mind, while *Some Thoughts Concerning Education* had detailed the many pitfalls and difficulties to be met by the skilled tutor in the effort to bring the youngster to reason and personhood. With knowledge enough to know their Maker and their duties, with reason constructing a polity concerned with the material and civic well-being of its members, men should not be troubled that other kinds of knowledge, 'the vast Ocean of Being' exceeded their grasp.[4] And should they, for whatever reason, find themselves incapable of defining a demonstrable science of morality through the use of unassisted reason, there was always recourse to be found in the Word of God, read and interpreted plainly as Locke had done for himself in *The Reasonableness of Christianity* and in *A Paraphrase*.

One might set rigorous controls over one's financial and material estate, but prescribing the terms of an intellectual legacy is another matter entirely. Many of those who claimed Locke's intellectual mantle, in Europe and in America, had little use for his theological orientation, his vision for a Christian England. The effusive Paul Hazard, writing in homage to the Locke of the Enlightenment mind, declared in 1935 that 'Locke stands at the turning point whence the

roads of Europe start for the New Age'.[5] But while Locke's advocacy of
toleration and individual autonomy was at the nucleus of the Enlightenment spirit, his fundamental concern with the fact of human
sinfulness and the essential work of a personal redeemer was erased
from public memory. The *Essay*'s disparagement of man's intellectual
potential was overlooked in favour of the book's implicit endorsement
of the progressive nature of knowledge, its renunciation of an ancient
wisdom lost at the Fall but available again (for a few) through the
inward working of the spirit. Locke's position on education became for
some during the course of the eighteenth century an endorsement of
nurture as the single criterion for successful socialization, overlooking
his consideration of the role of individual temperament and natural
bias, and minimizing the power of the irrational appetites and
passions. Finally, Locke's politics was often disengaged from his
broader Christian purpose, the natural law losing its bond with the
will of a supreme lawgiver and instead finding its anchor first in eternal
reason and at last in mere social and economic utility. The eighteenth-
century figures who claimed Locke's ideas as their own may not have
been concerned to master 'the vast Ocean of Being' referred to in the
introduction to the *Essay*, but neither were they, by and large, content
to restrict their inquiries to matters which concern conduct in the
interests of eternal felicity with the God of historic Christianity. Locke
had struggled to reintroduce that God to his contemporaries in a
primitive context of love and forgiveness, where the early apostles
communicated a message full of promise and simple trust. Sinners were
forgiven; reconciliation was at hand. With such clumsy and distracting
myths whose only purport was to distract enlightened man from the
urgent task of temporal reconstruction, the *philosophes* of the eighteenth
century would have nothing to do.

Looking at the publishing history of Locke's works in the century
after his death, it is obvious that there was much interest in and
discussion of his ideas. With the expansion of the middle-class reading
public during the course of the eighteenth century, Locke's ideas
touched a large audience. Richard Steele and Joseph Addison kept
many of these ideas in prominent view in issues of *The Tatler*, *Spectator*,
and *Guardian* between 1709 and 1713. Offering sympathetic expositions
of Locke's views on judgement, fancy, abuse of language, imagination,
duration and time, personal identity, and other topics, readers were
afforded the opportunity to consider Locke's anti-authoritarian sensibility. The *Essay* was a very popular book indeed throughout the
eighteenth century. As we have seen, four editions appeared between

its initial publication and Locke's death in 1704, and he was at work on a fifth edition at the end of his life. By 1786 the nineteenth edition had made its debut, and in addition to the complete text, over a dozen abridged versions would find their way into the bookshops. During the course of the century the *Essay* would be translated into French, German, Latin, together with abridgments in Italian and Greek. John Wynne's abridgment of the *Essay*, undertaken with Locke's approval in 1696 and designed with the undergraduate reader in mind, sold well throughout the century, with an American edition printed in 1794, nine years before the first American edition of the complete work.[6] Even before that first American edition, the work was being taught by instructors at Yale (1720) and at King's College (Columbia), and the College of Philadelphia before mid-century. One modern scholar has estimated that the *Essay* was owned by more Englishmen than the works of any other philosopher, and this all before Locke's death.[7] Over a dozen English printings of *A Letter Concerning Toleration* were issued, with Voltaire presenting a French translation in 1764, while *The Reasonableness of Christianity* appeared in a seventh edition during the same year. Similarly, a sixth edition of *Two Treatises* was available by 1764, and by the end of the century over two dozen editions and reprintings, including a French translation, were in the shops. Some of these reprints contained only the constructive Second Treatise, a reflection of the decline of patriarchal theory in the period. A three-volume set of Locke's *Works* was published for the first time in 1714, and a ten-volume tenth edition was published in 1801. Finally, *Some Thoughts Concerning Education* reached a fifteenth edition in 1778, and by that date it had been translated into Dutch, French, German, and Italian in multiple editions.[8]

The main appeal of Locke during the eighteenth century, most observers agree, was due to the widespread belief that he had successfully applied the empirical method of the natural sciences to the study of the mind based upon experience and observation. The result, it was believed, was a step-by-step analysis of the workings of the mind, from the first sensory experiences to the formation of complex ideas through the process of reflection. In eighteenth-century philosophy, Locke had given the world a 'history of the mind', contributing to the disenchantment of the physical world undertaken with such great success by his friend and fellow biblical exegete, Isaac Newton. In setting strict limits to our power to know, the *Essay* encouraged men to avoid the fruitless wrangle of traditional metaphysics, and described in clear terms the process by which we come to know what our faculties allow us to penetrate. Locke was called 'the ingenious Director of modern Philosophy' by a sympathetic Isaac Watts in 1733, and it was understood that his abolition of innate ideas was perhaps the strongest weapon in the arsenal assembled to put an end to all claims to epistemic authority which lay at the heart of *ancien régime* thought.[9] No more privileged access to special truths, no more unexamined superstition, no more divine right dogmatics; in Locke's radical epistemology, knowledge – even knowledge of God's word – must begin *de novo*, must be open to all because it is entirely drawn from direct sensation and interior reflection, from individual experience. According to G. R. Cragg in a still influential work published in 1964, 'the philosophy of the new age was launched on the side of vigorous protest against any disposition' not originating in the mind of the sovereign individual.[10] Thanks to Locke, sovereignty – intellectual, religious, political – had been returned to its original masters, those who would use the gift of reason intended for them by their Maker.

One of the most widely acknowledged contributions made by Locke to advocates of liberal reform across Europe and America in the eighteenth century was his lifelong promotion of what we would now call social environmentalism, the belief that a person's character is largely or even entirely the product of association, upbringing, circumstances. Related to this position is the notion that social condition or context is foundational to the happy and virtuous person. The social, political and legal institutions of a country, if erected and operated according to the principles of universal reason, will obviate the force of tendentious opinion, prejudice, and all forms of intolerance. Together with Locke's claim that differences among human beings are largely the result of social milieu, and his emphasis on the basic equality of a humanity which for centuries had been declared inherently unequal by virtue of the accidents of birth and inheritance, the new century had at its disposal a powerful intellectual tool for use against the myriad conceits of the *ancien régime*.

Sometimes lost within this assembly of ideas during the eighteenth century, however, was the Lockean qualification that constructive change should proceed from the enlightened education of the individual, not through the immediate and revolutionary transformation of existing institutions. Locke's environmentalism, in other words, was aimed specifically at reforming education within the current social and political order. Many of the *philosophes* who followed in the eighteenth century, particularly those in France who were alienated from the culture of the ruling classes, called for more sweeping changes, in some cases nothing less than the radical and immediate reshaping of all institutions.[11] For men like Helvetius, Condillac, Holbach, and Condorcet, state and society had to be transformed before individuals could be recreated; for these men collective social engineering took precedence over individual education. Helvetius, for example, thought that 'it may not be possible to make any considerable change in public education without making changes in the very constitution of the state'.[12] We should never forget that Locke was a member of the ruling elite, a comfortable property owner who had a considerable material stake in preserving existing institutions and social relations. This could be best accomplished, he thought, by practising the type of education conducive to intellectual self-direction, by erasing the tyranny of unquestioned authority without first overturning the established social and political arrangement.

The influence of Locke's educational ideas on the eighteenth century has been described by one modern scholar as 'monumental' with authors treating Locke's work as 'sacrosanct'.[13] In his recognition of childhood as a distinct stage in the psychological development of the morally responsible person, in calling for a new pedagogical style consistent with the physical, emotional and intellectual needs of unique individuals, Locke anticipated the experiential and non-didactic approach of enlightened eighteenth-century educators. Chamber's *Cyclopaedia* in 1738, under the heading 'education' asserted tersely that 'Mr. Locke's excellent treatise of education, is known to every body'. By the middle of the century, we are told, no author of a book on education could avoid reference to, and praise for, the contribution of Locke, who, unlike his Calvinist predecessors, did not believe that 'the end of all education was the perception of religious truth' – a measure of just how remote Locke's intentions had become for the eighteenth-century mind.[14]

But what then was the actual nature of that contribution for an eighteenth-century audience? What impact did those who pointed to Locke for inspiration and direction have upon the process of formal education in Europe and America? And what became of Locke's deep-seated belief that education into freedom was but a preliminary to 'Hopes of Acceptance and Reward' after death? What became of his conviction, expressed succinctly in the essay 'Of Study' that 'Heaven being our great business and interest, the knowledge which may direct us thither is certainly so, too; so that this is without peradventure the study which ought to take up the first and chiefest place in our thoughts'? [15]

In the first place, it is useful to recognize that there were voices of dissent, at least with respect to Locke's curricular priorities. John Clark, for example, writing 16 years after Locke's death and 27 years after the initial appearance of *Some Thoughts Concerning Education*, claimed that Locke's book was the only title on the subject worth the attention of the serious educator. And he praised Locke's *Essay* in his subsequent *Essay Upon Study* as the best source for the guidance and direction of the mind in its search after truth, directing students to read it over twice. But despite this more general endorsement, Clark took exception to Locke's emphasis on training for virtue and insisted that subject matter was equally important in the gentleman's education. Familiarity with the Latin language, knowledge of history and the law of nations, divinity and mathematics, all combined to direct virtue into constructive channels, whereas Locke's design to rectify the will was vulnerable to the designs of those who would inculcate false notions of duty.[16]

While the anti-patriarchal position adopted by Locke in the *Second Treatise* helped to alter the nature of parental authority and familial relations in general, there is little evidence to suggest that the Charity or Free schools which were founded in eighteenth-century England had any use for Locke's radical notion of the autonomous individual. Both opponents of any form of education for the poor, and defenders of the rudimentary training made available in the charity establishments, were interested primarily in buttressing the existing social hierarchy, finding the most effective means of instilling a due sense of subordination, of keeping the labouring poor from idleness and crime. 'Charity-Children', wrote W. Hendley in 1735, 'are taught to do their Duty in that State of Life, into which it shall please God to call them.' In *An Essay on the Government of Children* (1756), James Nelson confirmed that while the working poor were essential to the good of society, by 'the Wisdom of Providence' they had been born 'rather to Labour than to Idleness; to be obedient to the Laws, than to be Dispensers of them'.[17] Isaac Watts, whose praise for Locke's *Essay* was earnest, thought that the ability to read the Bible was essential to the well-being of the poor, and recommended they receive instruction in reading for at least two hours each day.[18] But Watts also believed that the new Lockean pedagogy had too often become an inducement to filial disobedience and licence. In his popular work on education, *The Improvement of the Mind* (1741), Watts lamented that 'in this century when the doctrine of a just and reasonable liberty is better known, too many of the present youth break all the bonds of nature and duty and run into the wildest degrees of looseness both in belief and practice'.[19] The 'virtues' of meekness, humility, decorum and subordination were those which the charity schools thought essential to the well-being of eighteenth-century society. Nevertheless, some observers disagreed with the entire charity school programme, and their dissent was based on what they took to be good Lockean principle. Bernard de Mandeville's critique of charity schools in his 1723 edition of *The Fable of the Bees*, for instance, highlighted Locke's concern for the education of the gentleman over the common labourer. 'Thinking and reasoning justly, as Mr. Locke has rightly observed, require time and practice.' Mandeville insisted that poor people 'that have not used themselves to thinking but just on their present necessities, make poor work of it when they try beyond that'.[20]

Some 25 years ago, in a remark on *Some Thoughts* that has largely gone unnoticed, Lawrence Cremin observed that while Locke's ped-agogical advice is often placed within the tradition of Renaissance civility primers, there is a perspective from which the book could be viewed chiefly as a devotional manual, that indeed this is how some of Locke's eighteenth-century popularizers utilized it. Instilling virtue, without which Locke believed 'he will be happy neither in this, nor the other world' involved preparing the student for a life worthy of eternal reward.[21] In books authored by the Dissenters Isaac Watts, James Burgh, and Philip Doddridge in the first half of the eighteenth century, the Lockean model of simple piety and virtuous living as the goal of education and the key to immortality made its way into the American colonial classroom. For Doddridge, piety was defined in his *Sermons on the Religious Education of Children* (1732, first colonial edition 1763) as the practice of benevolence, diligence, integrity, self-denial, and obedience to parents, all in the spirit of Locke's call for virtue in *Some Thoughts*. Burgh's *Thoughts on Education* (1747, first colonial edition 1749) admonished parents to treat their children as rational creatures, and sought to provide the student with practical skills for success in this life. Burgh thought that the twin goals of education involved the communication of a body of knowledge which would enable everyone 'to pass decently and comfortably through the present life', and, more importantly, directions on 'how to prepare himself for the everlasting duration after this life is at an end'.[22] Burgh was a Presbyterian, but he applauded Locke's *Reasonableness of Christianity* as one of the best guides available on the nature of true religion. And while Burgh, Doddridge, and Watts continued to write about the horrible consequences of eternal punishment for the damned in a manner alien to Locke's

Reasonableness, their emphasis upon the primacy of a working and socially active Christian virtue as the only legitimate measure of piety suggests that a prominent component of Locke's contribution to eighteenth-century educational thought lay in his affirmation of the value of otherworldly concerns and in his thoughts on the most efficacious means for attaining eternal reward. His concern with hardiness and self-denial, with reason over imagination, was not lost upon educational theorists who applauded both Locke's placement of example and encouragement before precept and rebuke, and his recommendation that the foundation of virtue is to be found in the early inculcation of 'a true Notion of God . . . Author and Maker of all Things, from whom we receive all our Good, who loves us, and gives us all Things'.[23] When the Anglican clergyman Richard Shepard wrote in 1782 that 'virtue is the main object of education' and that without it 'all the learning of the world will render us neither of use or ornament' the priorities established in *Some Thoughts* respecting conduct and piety found a sympathetic home.[24]

Locke's religious convictions, and the implications of his epistemology for religion, where authentic knowledge was restricted to the phenomenal realm, continued to occasion intense debate after his death and well into the eighteenth century. Over 20 authors with clerical affiliations, most of whom were High Church Anglicans or non-jurors, had taken exception to Locke's views in the ten years between 1697 and 1707, but the author had responded to only four of these critics at the time of his death. In 1697 the Grand Jury of Middlesex presented as a nuisance *The Reasonableness of Christianity* on the grounds that it denied the Trinity and forwarded Arianism, Socinianism, atheism, and Deism. Respecting Locke's *Reasonableness of Christianity* and Toland's *Christianity Not Mysterious*, William Carroll wrote in 1706 that 'Those two titles are different in Sound, but agree in Sense; as the two Books themselves do, in one and the same Design.'[25] The alleged design, of course, was to reduce God's intentions and His workings to the level of human reason, to jettison Scripture because it had become superfluous to the religion of reason. By 1730 Matthew Tindal's *Christianity as Old as the Creation* had brought the Deist argument to its disturbing (for the orthodox) conclusion, arguing that God's perfect handiwork revealed his intentions quite plainly, and that textual supplements like the Bible only implied that the workman was an imperfect communicator. While Locke had his defenders in print, as late as 1742 his epistemological doctrines were still being held responsible for the multiple errors of Deism.[26]

Doubtless a large part of the criticism directed at Locke's theology by members of the Established Church was motivated by their professional distaste for the view that each church was a voluntary association, one where faith was a matter between God and the individual. Together with his conviction that no man, much less any national institution, possessed the entire truth about matters of eternal concern, Locke's radical autonomy in religious affairs made his work unacceptable to the Church he claimed as his own. But it was, more than anything else, Locke's denial of innate knowledge and his elision of the massively learned resources of seventeenth-century theology that most alarmed his clerical contemporaries. It was easy to associate such a man with the flood of heterodox and anticlerical books which appeared on the market after the lapsing of the Licensing Act in 1695. Bishop Gilbert Burnet spoke for more than a few of his episcopal colleagues when he lamented that it now 'became a common topic of discourse to treat all mysteries in religion as the contrivances of priests to bring the world into a blind submission to them; priestcraft grew to be another word in fashion, and the enemies of religion vented all their impieties under the cover of these words.'[27]

One of the more unfortunate ways in which Locke's religious sensibility was distorted was in the extrapolation of his casual suggestion about thinking matter into the claim that he was, like the notorious Thomas Hobbes, a materialist. Locke's suggestion, made in Book 4 of the *Essay*, that matter might think, elicited a number of spirited criticisms throughout the course of the eighteenth century in Britain.[28] When he initially mentioned that 'We have the ideas of matter and thinking, but possibly shall never be able to know whether any mere material being think or no', Locke was seeking simply to illustrate the limits of human knowledge and not to challenge belief in the soul's immateriality. One cannot deny, he remarked, that God in His omnipotence 'has not given to some system of matter, fitly disposed, a power to perceive and think, or else joined and fixed to matter, so disposed, a thinking immaterial substance'.[29] Voltaire, in his *Letters Concerning the English Nation* (1733) recognized that Locke was making the point that we do not know how matter operates since all of our knowledge is based upon ideas and he poured scorn upon Locke's detractors. But when Voltaire proceeded to compare the human soul to a clock in the same essay, the analogy to mechanism could not have been more inappropriate.[30] By the last quarter of the century, Joseph Priestly was chiding Locke for having neither the courage nor the conviction to explode the immaterialist hypothesis when he had the opportunity.[31]

Preachers also continued to take issue in public sermons with Locke's notion that the same body is not essential to the idea of resurrection. In Easter sermons at Oxford University in 1711, 1720 and 1725, Locke's attempt to distinguish between the material body and its resurrection counterpart was condemned as heretical.[32] Catherine Cockburn, who had first written a defence of the *Essay* in 1702, responded in print to one of these sermons in 1726, but the preacher, Winch Holdsworth, vigorously defended his allegation that Locke's position qualified the philosopher as a dangerous Socinian.[33] By 1733, when one of the best known writers of the day, Isaac Watts, took up the issue as part of his *Philosophical Essays*, Locke's intentions were still a subject of much debate. Watts acknowledged this 'warm Dispute among Men of Learning', outlined the main biblical arguments put forward by the contending parties, and concluded that 'the Arguments on both Sides have some real Strength in them'. He offered a compromise where just so many of the same particles of the body constitute the raised man, 'some original, essential, and constituent tubes, Fibres or staminal particles' which remain the same throughout life.[34] Watts did not conclude that Locke was a mortalist who thought that consciousness ceased with the death of the body, but he acknowledged that mortalists 'who also go a step further' had successfully implicated Locke in their unacceptable picture of the afterlife.

Still Locke's appeal to the reasonable nature of Christian belief had a profound impact on the life of the official Church throughout the course of the eighteenth century. Apologists for traditional belief were confident that orthodoxy could meet the test of reason; everyone accepted the legitimacy of natural religion. 'Destroy the principles of reason', warned William Sherlock, 'and there is no room left for revelation.'[35] What remained in doubt was the degree to which the religion of nature was sufficient to the task of facilitating salvation. However much it distrusted the supposed intentions of the messenger, the eighteenth-century Church of England embraced Locke's position that God could not be comprehended in His entirety by mere human intellect. They insisted, like Locke, that there were truths above the reach of human faculties but consistent with eternal reason, 'truths' which the Deists associated with disingenuous New Testament authors and, more recently, with self-interested priestcraft. Similarly, Locke's conclusion that Revelation communicated truths and provided an unrivalled inducement to act in accordance with them was adopted by Anglican apologists who, like Locke, found natural theology to be defective in terms of providing motives to life-saving behaviour.

Locke's call for religious freedom in the *Letter on Toleration* was brought to fruition in certain limited respects in May 1689. After dismissing King William's call for a comprehension bill that would attract moderate Dissenters to the Church of England, Parliament passed a bill 'for exempting Their Majesties' Protestant subjects, dissenting from the Church of England, from the penalties of certain laws'.[36] Later known as the Toleration Act, the measure was largely an expedient response to actions taken by the Catholic King James II after 1685 when a calculated and cynical royal grant of toleration to Catholics and Dissenters had placed the Established Church in clear danger. Even Tory statesmen like Daniel Finch, Earl of Nottingham, supported the 1689 Toleration Act as an appropriate means of maintaining the future allegiance of Protestant Dissenters. Philipp van Limborch wrote to Locke in April 1689 praising the anonymous *Epistola de Tolerantia* and recommending it to members of Parliament. Anyone who was not persuaded by its arguments, Limborch observed, was 'not to be led by reason but to be carried headlong either by blind prejudice or by concern for their own advantage'.[37] It was an eerily prescient statement.

The toleration granted by the bill was not only disappointing to many English Dissenters, but to the professed Anglican John Locke as well. None of the laws against Dissenters was actually abolished; only the enforcement of penalties against dissent was suspended, provided that the non-Anglicans announced their allegiance to the new King and Queen. Roman Catholics were excluded from the bill, as were anti-Trinitarians – something of obvious concern to Locke. In addition, all Dissenters remained subject to the Test Act and the Corporation Act, which in law prevented non-Anglicans from serving in any municipal or political office, tithes continued to be assessed for the support of the Church of England, and the two universities continued to deny admission to anyone who was not a member of the official communion. Apprising Limborch of the results in Parliament, Locke acknowledged that politics was indeed the art of the possible. The toleration bill was not 'so wide in scope as might be wished for by you and those like you who are true Christians and free from ambition or envy. Still, it is something to have progressed so far.'[38] This was very much an understatement given the fact that no European state in the late seventeenth century was without an Established Church, and that no Established Church before this time had ever considered a modicum of toleration to those who dissented from it.[39]

Locke hoped that with the limited Toleration Act as a start, 'the foundations have been laid of that liberty and peace in which the

Church of Christ is one day to be established'.[40] In the century
following his death, however, little was accomplished in England in
terms of extending the small freedoms realized in 1689. In fact during
the reign of Queen Anne (1702–14) High Church clergy and their
Tory allies in Parliament attempted to roll back the concessionary
exemptions afforded Trinitarian Protestants after the flight into exile
of James II. Outraged by the practice of occasional conformity by
which prominent Dissenters attended Anglican services and took
communion once a year in order to qualify for civil and political
office, the cry against moderation was led by Dr Sacheverell in the
pulpit and by Francis Atterbury in the lower house of Convocation.
And although the terms of the Toleration Act were not repealed by a
Tory-dominated Parliament, the Whigs who came to power after the
death of the Queen did nothing substantive to improve the status of
Dissenters. The Test and Corporation Acts remained in place, anti-
trinitarians continued to be excluded from the terms of the toleration,
and the penalties against all forms of dissent (although not applied)
remained in law as a reminder to all that circumstances could change
for the worse should non-Anglicans press their demands too hard.
While a broad *de facto* toleration had witnessed the growth of Unitarianism during the course of the eighteenth century, the continuance
of the Toleration Act assumed that an official Church, in alliance with
Parliament, enjoyed the right to set the terms of one's religious
practice. The reaction occasioned by the excesses of the French
Revolution delayed the recognition of full equal rights for another
40 years, when those at the bottom of Locke's list of deserving subjects
– Roman Catholics – were finally emancipated in an effort to maintain
the stability of Empire on the other side of the Irish sea. It would not
be until the middle of the nineteenth century that Locke's vision of a
pluralist society, one where each individual is free to pursue his own
salvation without hindrance and without civil penalties, would be
secured. And by the time the vision had become a reality, Locke's
God-centred understanding of the human drama was well on its way
to becoming a quaint anachronism for the majority of English men
and women.

What of the effect of Locke's simple but revolutionary claim in his
Two Treatises that men's political obligations were not to be set by their
purported natural superiors, that the structure of authority was not in
a condition of permanent and divinely ordered stasis, that the political
structure could in fact be changed by men of property while avoiding
social insurrection and political instability from below? Interestingly

enough, the *Two Treatises of Government* did not face critical comment in print until 14 years after its initial appearance. The English journals of the period did not review or take much notice of the book, while most Whigs in the 1690s relied upon the arguments contained in works such as James Tyrrell's *Patriarcha Non Monarcha* (1680) or Algernon Sydney's *Discourses Concerning Government* (1698) for their defence of the Revolution of 1688–9, both of whose theories anticipated the ones contained in *Two Treatises*. Locke's book was not ignored by any means, but it was but one of a number of works embraced by advocates of constitutional government.[41] On at least one occasion the *Two Treatises* was utilized by the forces of Irish separatism, hardly an advertisement for the work likely to endear it to the conscience-troubled minds of the supporters of William and Mary. William Molyneux's *The Case of Ireland's being Bound by Acts of Parliament in England, Stated* (1698) called for Protestant Ireland's natural right to legislative independence, refuting England's claims to the island by right of conquest. The book was reprinted nine times between 1706 and 1782, and its author was much admired by Protestant proponents of an independent Irish Parliament.[42] Only after the English Revolution seemed secure did the radical doctrine of the *Second Treatise* gain in reputation, and only then in the context of legitimizing the removal of James II in 1688. As the more famous *Essay* gained in prestige during the second half of the eighteenth century, Locke's work on government was elevated, if for no other reason than the fact that the great philosopher had written a work advocating revolution. By the last quarter of the century, however, as Locke's doctrine came to be embraced by elements in society who wished to upset the comfortable social and political status quo – American revolutionaries and the emerging British working class – criticism of Locke as a dangerous subversive began in earnest.

Locke's place in eighteenth-century American colonial political discourse has been the subject of intense debate among scholars over the past 35 years, and there is no sign that a consensus is about to emerge any time soon. Prior to 1960 most scholars accepted without much qualification the key role of *Two Treatises* and of Locke's liberalism in general in the American founding. Toleration, individual rights, the protection of property, and the right to popular revolution were at the axis of the revolutionary experience, and Locke's formulation of these concepts, familiar to educated Americans, became the touchstone for all discussion with British imperial authorities. He was declared 'America's philosopher' by one commentator in the 1930s, while others assured more than one generation of university students that: 'It is not too much to say that during the era of the American Revolution, the "party line" was John Locke.'[43] Even broader claims were made in 1955 when Louis Hartz argued in his influential *Liberal Tradition in America* that Lockean liberalism had defined not only revolutionary debate but all subsequent American political thought and behaviour.

But a profound reassessment of this orthodoxy began around 1960, when a new generation of scholars claimed that there was little textual basis for the argument in favour of Locke's influence beyond its proponents' dubious claims of an unwritten Lockean 'climate of opinion' in America. This revisionist historiography has attempted to alter America's historical self-understanding by denying the importance of Locke's liberalism and replacing it with a picture of virtue-seeking citizen-farmers whose interest in themselves was uniformly put to one side for the good of the collective whole. Caroline Robbins was the first scholar to challenge the traditional 'Lockean' account of the origins of the American founding and to inaugurate what has come to be known as the school of 'republican revisionism'. In her book *The Eighteenth-Century Commonwealthman* (1959) Robbins discounted the influence of Locke's ideas in America and instead stressed the importance of opposition thought in London during the 1760s, when a group of 'Country' politicians challenged the perceived corruption of 'Court' interests who defended heavy taxation, a standing army, and government influence in the House of Commons. The so-called 'Real Whigs' within the Country opposition looked back to commonwealth writers such as John Milton, James Harrington and Algernon Sydney in their efforts to prevent the return of royal absolutism. According to Robbins, and subsequently Bernard Bailyn and Gordon Wood, the 'Real Whig' tradition of civic virtue and service against commercialism and corruption shaped the political consciousness of colonial leaders as they responded to imperial innovations after 1763.[44] Lockean individualism and natural rights were alien and unwanted ideas in an America where their attachment to the land protected the colonists from the corrupting influence of city and trade, the debilitating disease of political place and profit. Tyranny and corruption could only be avoided by separation from the source of the sickness.[45]

John Pocock traced this eighteenth-century colonial concern with the virtuous, other-regarding and independent citizen back to an even earlier source: the civic humanism of Aristotle, fifteenth-century Florence, the sixteenth-century thought of Machiavelli. In the Italian city-states of the fifteenth century, in Britain and in America in the eighteenth century, the focus was on the creation of workable mixed constitutions where the self-effacing and anti-capitalist civic spirit could flourish, where active citizenship and concern for the community promoted the development of the human personality, and, finally, where political decay and corruption could be arrested. Virtue, not commerce, the good of the whole, not the narrow interests of the individual and egocentric material accumulation, were always the paramount considerations.[46] Lockean liberalism and empiricism, his concern for the primacy of the atomistic individual and his approval of expanding commercial society, were marginalized by the revisionist scholars and displaced as the catalytic ideas behind the American founding. It was even concluded that few Americans had as much as read the *Two Treatises* before mid-century, even in the universities. Locke may have been claimed by the revolutionaries during the 1760s and 1770s, but mostly in order to attach a famous and generally respected name to political conclusions already reached on different grounds, not to provide initial inspiration. John Adams, for example, confessed to having read Harrington, Sydney, Hobbes and Locke before 1775, 'but with very little Application to any particular Views: till these Debates in Congress'.[47]

The revisionist effort to remove Locke from the story of American revolutionary intentions relies upon a picture of Lockean liberalism which is sharply at odds with the thesis contained in the foregoing chapters. In other words, the revisionist portrait of Lockean man – commercial, egocentric, concerned exclusively with immediate gratification and devoid of interest in the hereafter – has more to do with efforts to sanitize the intentions of the revolutionary generation, to free America's founders from venal interests, than it has to do with a sensitive reading of Locke's texts. In this respect it shares assumptions about Locke's disengagement from religion first put forward by Leo Strauss in his *Natural Right and History* (1953), a work which identifies Locke as an enemy of traditional religion. For the revisionists, Locke has no religious project, no trans-earthly paradigm by which human behaviour is to comport itself. Removing Locke's influence from the American founding presupposes, among other things, that his politics is divorced from his religion and that his God does not set general duties which can only be realized in civil society. The revisionist's Locke is unconcerned with civic virtue because bourgeois man has no use for the moral prescriptions and prohibitions of traditional Christianity. The majority of colonists, it is claimed, were concerned with aligning their thought and action with Christian precepts, thus to separate Locke from this perspective makes the case for denying his influence in eighteenth-century America quite manageable.

The Locke presented in the preceding chapters, however, the man who linked politics with a larger Christian purpose, was very much a presence in eighteenth-century America. As Steven Dworetz has most recently argued, one can locate the influence of Locke's political thought most clearly in the works of the New England clergy, men who were obviously concerned about the moral implications of political action, and men who, like the Locke ignored in revisionist literature, placed every discussion of politics within the context of one's eternal destiny.[48] The New England clergy played a prominent role in the effort to raise popular opposition to British imperial actions after 1763. Locke's doctrine of consent, toleration, the limits of lawful government, and the nature of representation all find voice in the pamphlet and sermon literature of the 1760s and 1770s, although only those historians and political scientists opposed to the now fashionable 'republican revisionism' have begun to present the textual evidence for a Lockean connection in this area.[49] Locke was commonly cited by ministers who denounced passive obedience as an affront to both reason and Revelation, and from the pulpit the right and duty of resistance were often couched in Lockean language respecting the preservation of property as the proper end of civil government. Like Locke, clergymen insisted that individual judgement in religion must be extended to the political arena if mankind were to fulfil its obligation to respect the law of nature; every person must judge for himself if obedience to the commands of the magistrate are warranted by natural law. Liberty in religious and political affairs alone can assure that each person can act as a responsible agent in a moral universe defined by the Creator. When the Massachusetts minister Charles Turner declared in a sermon of 1773 that 'religious liberty is so blended with civil that if the one fails it is not to be expected that the other will continue', he was reaffirming the theological commitments of Locke's God-centred philosophy where individual autonomy and responsibility specified the appropriate comportment of mankind before its Maker. Similarly when Thomas Jefferson proclaimed 'upon the altar of God, eternal hostility to all forms of tyranny over the mind of man', he was reaffirming the call to personal independence situated at the heart of *An Essay Concerning Human Understanding*.[50] Allowing such tyranny, acquiescing in the systematic denial of elemental human

rights, could under no circumstances comport with the highest divine
mandate for humankind.

The Unitarian Jefferson, who like the Unitarian Locke, remained a
lifetime communicant in a Church which owed its origins to the
authoritarian ambitions of the second Tudor monarch, could not
separate his anti-authoritarian political tenets from his most deeply
held religious convictions. That there could be no safety for individual
bodies under the dominion of a sovereign whose title originated in a
source other than consent, had by the late eighteenth century become
an axiom of colonial political thought; equally axiomatic was the belief
that there could be no safety for disobedient souls before a God who
had set specific purposes for his special creation. Locke had stated the
case plainly for anyone contemplating a particular course of action in
A Letter Concerning Toleration: 'there is nothing in this World that is of
any consideration in comparison with Eternity'.[51] Jefferson, not unlike
Locke, was prepared to defend his actions before 'the laws of nature
and nature's God', an entirely apposite position for a believing
Christian, no matter how heterodox his views. And like Locke, the
author of the Declaration of Independence held that the individual's
duty before God always took precedence over duty before mere human
or public authority. The distance travelled between the intellectual
presuppositions, the religious world-views, of the seventeenth-century
Englishman and the eighteenth-century American, was not, in the
end, altogether compelling, irrespective of recent efforts to make the
former's ideas and intentions simply irrelevant to the latter.

CONCLUSION

Locke's career might best be summarized as an unending campaign against moral and epistemological paternalism, the traditional and widely endorsed notion that superior others were charged by God to dictate the thought and action of subject humankind. In religion, in politics, in education, in common social relations, the medieval and early modern Christian inheritance had stressed that truths had already been established, that multilayered ranks of superintendents had been charged with both disseminating and enforcing these truths, and that stasis and unquestioning obedience to the established natural hierarchies in the field of human relations was the mandate of the divine architect. Locke, it appears, wished to broaden the initial Reformation emphasis on inner conviction and the equality of persons before God in order to encompass the entire spectrum of human connections. While always keen to defend existing disparities in the distribution of economic power when such power was the result of industry and application, Locke provided the late seventeenth century with a strong epistemic argument for the sameness of human nature, for the primacy of reason in defining adulthood, and in the process he dismantled the intellectual and moral underpinnings of the medieval social and political universe.

If even a portion of the above claims is defensible, then it would be hard to disallow Locke's significance for the intellectual history of the modern West. But even if we accept this summary characterization, we must still keep in mind what was for Locke, and for the overwhelming majority of his peers, the preliminary nature of obedience and its opposite in the realm of the flesh, the brief and troublesome moment on earth before the unending requital with the Father. Political life, social action, economic behaviour, religious praxis – all of the stages on which one performs between birth and the silence of the grave had for Locke only one meaningful reference point, and life without that reference point would be a life devoid of rules, a life without essential purpose. The God of reason who is always present in *Two Treatises*, in *An Essay Concerning Human Understanding*, in *Some Thoughts Concerning*

Education, indeed in all of Locke's published and unpublished reflections on the human drama, this God sets a universal moral agenda and requires obedience to it. Reason tells us what is right while God is the source of our obligation to act accordingly. The passing of individuals on the profane stage was important but preludial, while the death of every person inaugurated the penultimate scene, beyond the grasp of frail human reason, where anticipation of the final judgement defined one's identity, one's consciousness after the body had been abandoned.

It may be the case that these issues have ceased to engage all but the peripheral attention of the modern West; autonomy has been taken one very large step beyond the Lockean paradigm, with results over the past 300 years that one might describe as uneven at best. But whatever our estimate of the modern situation where self-mastery and self-definition have replaced an externally mandated intention, Locke's vision of individual autonomy presupposed a specific set of obligations as old as the Hebrew prophets and as inflexible as mortality itself. The familiar, if unloved, host of medieval superiors had been reduced by Locke to a set of self-imposed and entirely terrene legislators and executives, leaving only the God of Christianity as the one head who deserves unswerving obedience. Here was a message designed both to emancipate and to constrain, for in declaring counterfeit the great chain of being in the intellectual and political world, Locke had visited a tremendous new burden upon his contemporaries and his successors. Freedom within the confines of a knowable moral law, intention and application as the measure of one's worthiness for communion with Christ, the need for the common person to study, to interpret, and to obey the unadorned word spoken by the Son of God – these things demanded the type of application, the devotion to higher purpose, not altogether usual in Locke's day, or in ours. Locke's Christian England was very much interested in the amelioration of the human condition, but only in an instrumental manner, as a conduit to something beyond the selfish individualism that is too often associated with the Lockean inheritance.

At the heart of the early Protestant experience had been the primary assertion that belief was a personal matter, that no individual, regardless of his or her station in society, could speak for or mediate with God on behalf of another. During the years of Locke's youth, this principle had been taken by Seekers, Ranters, Muggletonians, Diggers, Anabaptists, the Family of Love, and Fifth Monarchists in directions guaranteed to disrupt established social, political and economic norms. The antinomian 'inner light', where Christ is in

men and where reason, together with the Revealed Word, stand as just
two more barriers to the sublime, had fostered conditions where even
the concept of sin itself came under attack, where 'true levellers' like
Gerrard Winstanley could claim political and economic democracy as
the mandate of God. Locke had welcomed the restoration of the Stuart
monarchy and had written in defence of conformity to the church
framework mandated by the prince because in the early 1660s he
feared that heterodoxy weakened the very foundations of civil society.
The sectaries had advanced one set of improbable epistemic claims
during the Interregnum, and these in turn were countered by another
set when the machinery of persecution was restarted by Gilbert
Sheldon's Church of England after 1660.

By 1665 neither formula comported with Locke's picture of human
nature as potentially rational and subject to a God whose every
requirement for humanity conforms to the voice of reason. Neither
the unregulated promptings of the spirit nor the demands of the
church and state powers that be could reconcile themselves with the
divine requirements for humankind. Locke's radical questioning of the
traditional foundations of belief, his call for mental, moral, and
personal liberty, for an end to all forms of intellectual and affective
bondage, was intended to strengthen the relationship between sinner
and saviour, to place the individual unaccompanied before God as
contemplated by the first reformers. The attainment of eternal happiness, he wrote in *A Letter Concerning Toleration*, 'can neither be facilitated by another man's industry, nor can the loss of it turn to another
man's prejudice, nor the hope of it be forced from him by any external
violence'. In a century where matters of the soul still merited the
attention of philosophers, where Augustine's 'City of God' continued
to take precedence over the evanescent city of man, the essence of
Locke's project was anything but innovative. 'Every man has an
immortal soul' and securing God's favour requires our utmost care,
'because there is nothing in this World that is of any consideration in
comparison with Eternity'.[1] If a less devout eighteenth century overlooked Locke's core intention for a set of otherwise laudable human
ends, such work need not deflect us from appreciating the richness and
the piety of the original design.

NOTES

Introduction

1. Michael Ayers, *Locke: Epistemology and Ontology*, 2 vols (New York, 1993), 1:113. Eldon Eisenach, 'Religion and Locke's Two Treatises', in Edward J. Harpham (ed.), *John Locke's Two Treatises of Government: New Interpretations* (Lawrence, KS, 1992), p. 73, argues that the *Essay* 'can be read as a handbook for Protestant Salvation, such was its twin insistence on the standards of reason and morality and on the necessity of faith'.
2. See Jonathan Scott, 'England's Troubles: Exhuming the Popish Plot', in Tim Harris, Paul Seaward, and Mark Goldie (eds), *The Politics of Religion in Restoration England* (Oxford, 1990), pp. 108–11.
3. For the 'long view' of the decline of church authority, see C. John Sommerville, *The Secularization of Early Modern England* (Oxford, 1992), pp. 165–77.
4. Theodore Rabb, *The Struggle for Stability in Early Modern Europe* (New York, 1975); Richard Bonney, *The European Dynastic States, 1494–1660* (Oxford, 1991). Bonney prefers to view the period as one in which dynastic power, not impersonal states where kingship was a mere office, was solidified with the support of society's elites.
5. Richard Quintana, *Two Augustans: Locke and Swift* (Madison, WI, 1978), p. 34; John Yolton, *Locke: An Introduction* (Oxford, 1985), p. 2; Ian Harris, *The Mind of John Locke: A Study of Political Theory in its Intellectual Setting* (Cambridge, 1994), p. 17.
6. The classic statement is Richard H. Tawney, *Religion and the Rise of Capitalism* (London, 1927).
7. See, for example, most recently Ulrich Im Hof, *The Enlightenment*, trans. William E. Yuill (Oxford, 1994), pp. 169, 206.
8. Richard Ashcraft, 'Faith and Knowledge in Locke's Philosophy', in John Yolton (ed.), *John Locke: Problems and Perspectives* (Cambridge, 1969), pp. 194–223, recognized the religious agenda informing Locke's work.
9. ECHU, 4.14.2.; ELN, 229 (Locke's valedictory address as censor of moral theology at Christ Church for 1664).
10. Wolterstorff, 'Locke's Philosophy of Religion', in Vere Chappell (ed.), *The Cambridge Companion to Locke* (Cambridge, 1994), p. 174.
11. Ashcraft, 'Faith and Knowledge', p. 194.
12. John Redwood, *Reason, Ridicule and Religion: The Age of Enlightenment in England, 1660–1750* (London, 1976), p. 9.
13. ECHU, Epistle to the Reader, 6; 1.1.5, 1.1.6.
14. *Second Vindication of the Reasonableness of Christianity* in *Works*, 7:358.
15. ECHU, 4.19.1.

1 A Life of Counsel

1. Maurice Cranston, *John Locke: A Biography* (London, 1957, 2nd edn Oxford, 1985), still provides good overall coverage. See also John Milton, 'Locke's Life and Times', in Chappell (ed.), *The Cambridge Companion to Locke*, pp. 5–25, for a brief but up-to-date entry. John Marshall's *John Locke: Resistance, Religion and Responsibility* (Cambridge, 1994), and Harris, *Mind of John Locke* (Cambridge, 1994) offer the most thorough and incisive treatments of Locke's intellectual development currently available.

2. E.G.W. Bill, *Education at Christ Church, Oxford, 1650–1800* (Oxford, 1988) provides the details on academic life in the university city. Locke's medical interests are described by P. Romanell, *John Locke and Medicine: A New Key to Locke* (Buffalo, NY, 1984), and by Kenneth Dewhurst, *John Locke, Physician and Philosopher: A Medical Biography* (London, 1963).

3. Le Clerc quoted in Richard Aaron, *John Locke* (Oxford, 1973), p. 5. For new insights into these years at Oxford, see J.R. Milton, 'Locke at Oxford', in G.A.J. Rogers (ed.), *Locke's Philosophy: Content and Context* (Oxford, 1994), pp. 29–47. I am indebted to Professor Milton's essay for the following overview.

4. Milton, 'Locke at Oxford', pp. 35–6.

5. Locke first met Boyle in 1660, and read each of Boyle's works as they were published. M.A. Stewart, 'Locke's Professional Contacts with Robert Boyle', *Locke Newsletter*, 12 (1981), 19–44; Milton, 'Locke at Oxford', pp. 35–6; W.M. Spellman, *John Locke and The Problem of Depravity* (Oxford, 1988), pp. 63–5.

6. Correspondence, 1:163.

7. Correspondence, 1:82.

8. Correspondence, 1:59.

9. Paul Seaward, *The Restoration, 1660–1688* (London, 1991), p. 2. Ronald Hutton, *The British Republic, 1649–1660* (London, 1990), pp. 114–32, discusses the crises facing republicans after the death of Cromwell.

10. Correspondence, 1:75.

11. Philip Abrams (ed.), *John Locke: Two Tracts on Government* (Cambridge, 1967), p. 220; Gordon Schochet, 'Toleration, Revolution and Judgment in the Development of Locke's Political Thought', *Political Science*, 40 (1988), 84–96.

12. *Two Tracts*, 120.

13. Richard Ashcraft, *Revolutionary Politics and Locke's 'Two Treatises of Government'* (Princeton, NJ, 1986) and *Locke's 'Two Treatises of Government'* (London, 1987). On Shaftesbury's career see K.H.D. Haley, *The First Earl of Shaftesbury* (Oxford, 1968).

14. Ashcraft acknowledges that Maurice Cranston first brought attention to the fact that Locke was politically engaged when writing his major works. See Cranston, 'The Politics of a Philosopher', *Listener* (5 Jan. 1961), 18. Both Peter Laslett, in his introduction to *Two Treatises of Government* (New York, 1965), pp. 37–50, and Ashcraft, *Revolutionary Politics*, pp. 83–7, emphasize the influence of Shaftesbury upon Locke's thought.

15. This overview of London is from Neal Wood, *The Politics of Locke's Philosophy* (Berkeley, CA, 1984), pp. 7–12.

16. Correspondence, 1:228.

17. Jean Le Clerc, *Life of Locke*, quoted in Laslett (ed.), *Two Treatises*, p. 39.

18. David Wootton (ed.), *Political Writings of John Locke* (New York, 1993), p. 37.

19. Four drafts of this essay were written by Locke. The one referred to here is printed in H.R. Fox-Bourne, *The Life of John Locke*, 2 vols (London, 1876), 1:174–94. Quote from p. 175.

20. G.A.J. Rogers, 'Locke and the latitude-men: Ignorance as a Ground of Toleration' in Richard Kroll, Richard Ashcraft and Perez Zagorin (eds), *Philosophy, Science, and Religion in England 1640–1700* (Cambridge, 1992), pp. 199–229.

21. Milton, 'Locke at Oxford', pp. 41–2.

22. On the latitudinarians see W.M. Spellman, *The Latitudinarians and the Church of England* (Athens, GA, 1993).

23. R. Latham and W. Matthews (eds), *The Diary of Samuel Pepys*, 11 vols (Berkeley, CA, 1977–83), 9:60.

24. John Marshall, 'Locke and Latitudinarianism', in *Philosophy, Science and Religion in England 1640–1700*, pp. 253–82, examines Locke's links with the broad-church divines. See also Spellman, *Locke and Depravity*, pp. 63–103.

25. Ashcraft, *Locke's Two Treatises of Government*, pp. 23–4. Wootton, *Political Writings of Locke*, p. 30, stresses that while Parker's book was important, Locke's decision to begin the *Essay* can be traced back to his earlier concerns, first voiced in the 1660s, with the problem of scepticism.

26. Wootton, *Political Writings*, p. 19, suggests that Locke may have been in France as a spy for the Whig opposition to Charles II, or due to the fact that he may have had a hand in the composition of the opposition pamphlet, *A Letter from a Person of Quality to His Friend in the Country* (1675) and feared for his safety.

27. On Exclusion, see John Miller, *Popery and Politics in England, 1660–1688* (Cambridge, 1973) and J.R. Jones, *The First Whigs: The Politics of the Exclusion Crisis* (London, 1961).

28. On the role of the crowd during the Exclusion crisis, see Tim Harris, *London Crowds in the Reign of Charles II* (Cambridge, 1987), pp. 96–129.

29. On the relationship between Tyrrell's book and Locke's manuscript, see Wootton, *Political Writings*, pp. 49–64. On their at times strained relationship see J.H. Gough, 'James Tyrrell: Whig Historian and Friend of Locke', *Historical Journal*, 19 (1976), 581–610.

30. Seaward, *Restoration*, p. 112.

31. Quoting Mark Goldie, 'John Locke's Circle and James II', *Historical Journal*, 35 (1992), 559.

32. Limborch to Damaris Masham, 10 Nov. 1704. Quoted in Fox Bourne, *Life of Locke*, 2:6.

33. Correspondence, 2:787.

34. Cranston, *John Locke*, p. 233; Spellman, *Locke and Depravity*, pp. 82–4.

35. John Miller, *James II* (Hove, Sussex, 1978) provides the best coverage of these events.

36. Maurice Cranston, 'John Locke and the Case for Toleration', in Susan Mendus and David Edwards (eds), *On Toleration* (Oxford, 1987), p. 106, reminds us of the larger European context in which Locke was writing at this time.

37. Halifax quoted in Seaward, *Restoration*, p. 133.

38. On Furly see W.I. Hull, *Benjamin Furly and Quakerism in Rotterdam* (Lancaster, PA, 1941); Cranston, *John Locke*, pp. 281–2.

39. Correspondence, 3:1120; 3:1147.

40. Correspondence, 3:1127.

41. See Arthur Wainwright's introduction to his edition of the *Paraphrase and Notes*, 2 vols (Oxford, 1987), especially 1:5,11.

42. See Mark Goldie, 'John Locke, Jonas Proast and Religious Toleration, 1688–1692', in J. Walsh, C. Haydon and S. Taylor (eds), *The Church of England, 1689–1833: From Toleration to Tractarianism* (Oxford, 1993), pp. 143–71.

43. Michael Hunter, '"Aikenhead the Atheist": The Context and Consequences of Articulate Irreligion in the Late Seventeenth Century', in Hunter and David Wootton (eds), *Atheism from the Reformation to the Enlightenment* (Oxford, 1992), pp. 221–54.

44. J.C.D. Clark, *English Society, 1688–1832* (Cambridge, 1985), p. 277.
45. John C. Biddle, 'Locke's Critique of Innate Ideas and Toland's Deism', *Journal of the History of Ideas*, 37 (1976), 411–22.
46. Correspondence, 5:1856.
47. Correspondence, 7:2742.
48. Correspondence, 6:2414.
49. Correspondence, 8:3435.
50. Locke to Collins, quoted in Cranston, *John Locke*, p. 461.

2 Knowledge, Duty and Salvation

1. See ECHU, 'Epistle to the Reader', 7. The early drafts have been most recently edited by P.H. Nidditch and G.A.J. Rogers, *Drafts for the Essay Concerning Human Understanding, and other philosophical writings* (Oxford, 1990).
2. ECHU, 1.1.5; 4.12.11.
3. See, most recently, J.A.I. Champion, *The Pillars of Priestcraft Shaken* (Cambridge, 1992); John Spurr, *The Restoration Church of England, 1646–1689* (New Haven, CT, 1993). Also Clark, *English Society, 1688–1832*.
4. Harris, *Mind of Locke*, pp. 165–6.
5. Locke's manuscript notes on Edward Stillingfleet's *Unreasonableness of Separation* (1680) quoted in Marshall, *John Locke*, p. 98.
6. Quoted in Richard Aaron and Jocelyn Gibb (eds), *An Early Draft of Locke's Essay, Together with Excerpts from His Journals* (Oxford, 1936), p. 88.
7. ECHU, 1.1.2. According to John Marshall, 'constructing a sufficient defence of man's ability to know the duties that he was required to perform was a fundamental reason for composition of the *Essay Concerning Human Understanding*'. Marshall, 'John Locke and Latitudinarianism', in *Philosophy, Science, and Religion*, pp. 261–2.
8. ELN, 136–45; John Dunn, *Locke* (Oxford, 1984), p. 62.
9. ECHU, 'Epistle to the Reader', 9.
10. For a discussion see Peter Walmsley, 'Dispute and Conversation: Probability and the Rhetoric of Natural Philosophy in Locke's Essay', *Journal of the History of Ideas*, 54 (1993), 381–94.
11. ECHU, 'Epistle to the Reader', 10.
12. John Yolton, *John Locke: An Introduction* (Oxford, 1985), p. 119.
13. John Yolton, *John Locke and the Way of Ideas* (Oxford, 1956), p. 31. See also J. B. Schneewind, 'Locke's Moral Philosophy', in *Cambridge Companion to Locke*, pp. 199–225.
14. Aquinas, *Summa Theologica*, 61 vols (London, 1963–76), 1a qu 93 art. 9.
15. James Tully, *An Approach to Political Philosophy: Locke in Contexts* (Cambridge, 1993), ch. 6.
16. ECHU, 1.4.24.
17. Ibid.
18. Burnet, *Remarks Upon an Essay Concerning Human Understanding in a Letter Addressed to the Author* (London, 1697), p. 5.
19. Culverwell, *An Elegant and Learned Discourse on the Light of Nature* (Toronto, 1971), p. 54. See also Ralph Cudworth, *Treatise Concerning Eternal and Immutable Morality* (London, 1739), and Henry Lee, *Anti-Skepticism* (London, 1702).
20. ECHU, 1.3.14.
21. *Two Tracts*, 138; ECHU, 1.3.8.
22. ECHU, 2.1.2.
23. For a discussion see Barbara Shapiro, *Probability and Certainty in Seventeenth-Century England* (Princeton, NJ, 1983) and H.G. van Leeuen, *The Pursuit of Certainty in English Thought* (The Hague, 1963).

24. ECHU, 4.15.1; 4.14.2.
25. ECHU, 4.20.6.
26. ECHU, 4.1.2; 4.4.3.
27. ECHU, 4.4.1.
28. Henry More, *The Immortality of the Soul*, Book 1, ch. 2, Axiom no.8 quoted in G.A.J. Rogers, 'Locke and the latitude-men: ignorance as a ground of toleration', in *Philosophy, Science and Religion in England*, p. 238.
29. Margaret J. Osler, 'John Locke and the Changing Ideal of Scientific Knowledge', *Journal of the History of Ideas*, 31 (1970), 3. See also G.A.J. Rogers, 'Boyle, Locke and Reason', *Journal of the History of Ideas*, 27 (1966), 205–16.
30. ECHU, 2.11.6.
31. ECHU, 4.4.6.
32. ECHU, 4.12.11; 3.11.16; 4.2.4.
33. ECHU, 4.12.8; 4.3.18.
34. ECHU, 1.3.7; 2.28.5. See also 2.28.8.
35. Correspondence, 4:1579.
36. John Colman, *John Locke's Moral Philosophy* (Edinburgh, 1983), p. 216. Cf. John Yolton, *Locke and the Compass of Human Understanding* (Cambridge, 1970), pp. 145–6. Vere Chappell, 'Locke on the Intellectual Basis of Sin', *Journal of the History of Philosophy*, 32 (1994), 197–207, sees intellectualist strains in the second edition of the *Essay*, although he acknowledges that Locke makes an important shift between 1689 and 1694.
37. ECHU, 2.21.35; 2.21.37; 1.3.13.
38. Tillotson quoted in W.M. Spellman, 'Archbishop John Tillotson and the Meaning of Moralism', *Anglican and Episcopal History*, 56 (1987), 411–12.
39. See, for example, letter from Molyneux dated 27 August 1692 in Correspondence, 4:1530. See also Locke's letter to Tyrrell, 4 August 1690, in Correspondence, 4:1309.
40. Paraphrase, 2: 499. For a discussion, see David Wootton, 'John Locke: Socinian or Natural Law Theorist?', in James E. Crimmins (ed.), *Religion, Secularization and Political Thought: Thomas Hobbes to J.S. Mill* (London, 1989), pp. 42–3.
41. 'Of Ethick in General' printed in Peter King, *The Life and Letters of John Locke* (London, 1884; reprinted London, 1984), pp. 308–9.
42. STCE, 321.
43. Works, 7:122, 139.
44. Ibid., 140.
45. Ibid., 140, 144.
46. John Yolton, *A Locke Dictionary* (Oxford, 1993), p. 77.
47. ECHU, 4.18.2. See also 4.16.14.
48. ECHU, 4.18.6; 4.18.10. Compare his 'Discourse on Miracles' in Works, 9:257 where he says 'To know that any revelation is from God, it is necessary to know that the messenger that delivers it is sent from God'.
49. Whichcote, *Moral and Religious Aphorisms*, ed. Samuel Salter (London, 1753), no.771.
50. ECHU, 4.19.12.
51. ECHU, 2.27.26.

3 The Heterodoxy of a Simple Faith

1. Works, 4:96; 4:341.
2. Paraphrase, 1:171.

3. Santayana, *Some Turns of Thought in Modern Philosophy* (New York, 1933), pp. 13–14.
4. ECHU, 4.14.2.
5. Richard Ashcraft, 'John Locke's Library: Portrait of an Intellectual', in Jean Yolton (ed.), *A Locke Miscellany* (Bristol, 1990), p. 227; John Harrison and Peter Laslett (eds), *The Library of John Locke* (Oxford, 1965).
6. Marshall, 'Locke and Latitudinarianism', p. 254; Milton, 'Locke at Oxford', pp. 41, 42; Mark Goldie, 'John Locke, Jonas Proast and Religious Toleration', in J. Walsh, C. Haydon, and S. Taylor (eds), *The Church of England 1689–1833: From Toleration to Tractarianism* (Cambridge, 1993), p. 144.
7. On the theology of the latitudinarians see W.M. Spellman, *The Latitudinarians and the Church of England, 1660–1700* (Athens, GA, 1993). See also, more generally, Gerard Reedy, *The Bible and Reason: Anglicans and Scripture in Late Seventeenth-Century England* (Philadelphia, 1985).
8. Marshall, *Locke*, pp. 119–25. Spellman, *Locke and Depravity*, pp. 63–103.
9. Redwood, *Reason, Ridicule and Religion*, p. 30.
10. Works, 7. 294.
11. John Yolton, *Thinking Matter: Materialism in Eighteenth-Century Britain* (Minneapolis, 1984), p. 3. Cf. Redwood, *Reason, Ridicule and Religion*, pp. 9–15.
12. Philip C. Almond, *Heaven and Hell in the English Enlightenment* (Cambridge, 1994), provides the most recent treatment of the subject. More general surveys include Philippe Aries, *The Hour of Our Death* (New York, 1981); and John MacManners, *Death and the Enlightenment* (New York, 1986).
13. For a discussion of seventeenth-century views of afterlife as expressed from the pulpit, see W.M. Spellman, 'Between Death and Judgment: Conflicting Images of the Afterlife in Seventeenth-Century English Eulogies', *Harvard Theological Review*, 87 (1994), 49–66 and idem, 'Almost Final Things: Jeremy Taylor and the Anglican Dilemma of the Dead Awaiting Resurrection', *Anglican and Episcopal History*, 63 (1994). A good general survey of Western views from antiquity is Colleen McDannell and Bernard Lang, *Heaven: A History* (New Haven, CT, 1988).
14. Burnet, *An Exposition of the Thirty-Nine Articles of the Church of England* (London, 1699), p. 221; Stevens, *Whole Parable of Dives and Lazarus* (London, 1697), p. 90.
15. Spellman, 'Between Death and Judgment', pp. 50–4.
16. Ray Anderson, *Theology, Death and Dying* (New York, 1984) p. 57; N.T. Burns, *Christian Mortalism from Tyndale to Milton* (Cambridge, MA, 1972) is still the best survey of mortalist thought in the seventeenth century.
17. Irenaeus quoted in Paul Badham, *Christian Beliefs About Life After Death* (London, 1976), p. 48. Aquinas, *Summa Theologica*, Book 1, Question 76, 'the unity of body and soul'.
18. R.C. Finucaane, 'Sacred Corpse, Profane Carrion: Social Ideals and Death Rituals in the Later Middle Ages', in Joachim Whaley (ed.), *Mirrors of Mortality: Studies in the Social History of Death* (New York, 1981), pp. 40–60.
19. Works, 7:9.
20. ECHU, 4.3.29, 4.18.7; *Second Reply*, in Works, 4: 333–4. See also Paraphrase, 2:684.
21. See Marshall, *Locke*, p. 154. 'Of Study' is printed in James Axtell (ed.), *The Educational Writings of John Locke* (Cambridge, 1968), p. 410.
22. Works, 4: 308.
23. Paraphrase, 1:252.
24. Paraphrase, 2:255 (Locke's paraphrase of 1 Corinthians VX.50).
25. ELN, p. 173.
26. *Reasonableness*, p. 149.
27. ECHU, 2.1.10–2.1.20. In 1.1.2 Locke announced that he would not examine wherein the essence of mind consists.
28. For a discussion see Garth Kemering, 'Locke on the Essence of Soul', *Southern Journal of Philosophy*, 17 (1979), 455–64.

29. ECHU, 4.3.6. On Stillingfleet, see Yotton, *Thinking Matter*, pp. 17–18.
30. Bentley, 'Matter and Motion Cannot Think', in Alexander Dyce (ed.), *The Works of Richard Bentley*, 3 vols (London, 1838), 3:45.
31. Works, 4:469.
32. David Wootton, 'New Histories of Atheism', in Hunter and Wootton (eds), *Atheism from the Reformation to the Enlightenment*, pp. 35–6, 48–9.
33. Works, 7:161.
34. H. McLachlan, *The Religious Opinions of Milton, Locke and Newton* (Manchester, 1941), p. 94; D.P. Walker, *The Decline of Hell: Seventeenth-Century Discussions of Eternnal Torment* (Chicago, 1964); Edwin Froom, *The Conditionalist Faith of Our Fathers* (Washington, DC, 1965).
35. Works, 7:7.
36. ECHU, 2.28.8; 2.21.70. See also *A Letter Concerning Toleration* ed. James Tully (Indianapolis, 1983), p. 24, where Locke speaks of 'eternal perdition'.
37. Milner, *Reflections on the Fourth Book of Mr. Locke's Essay* (London, 1700).
38. Paraphrase, 1:252. The paper 'Resurrectio et quae sequuntur' is printed in Paraphrase, 2:679–84.
39. ELN, 187.
40. In notes from 1680 on God's principal attributes, Locke acknowledged that misery was 'a worse state than annihilation, as pain is than insensibility'. See 'The Idea We Have of God' printed in Wootton (ed.), pp. 237–8.
41. Tillotson, 'The Christian Life, a Life of Faith', in *Works*, 10 vols (London, 1820), 4:188.
42. Works, 4:343.
43. Edwards, *Some Thoughts Concerning the Several Causes and Occasions of Atheism* (London, 1695).
44. ECHU, 4.3.18.
45. ECHU, 4.4.1.
46. ECHU, 4.19.4; 4.16.4; 4.18.4.
47. *Reasonableness of Christianity* in Works, 7:157.
48. *Reasonableness of Christianity* in Works, 7:146; Correspondence, 5:1538.
49. *Reasonableness* in Works, 7:147.
50. ECHU, 4.19.7.
51. ECHU, 4.18.8.
52. John Yolton, *John Locke: An Introduction*, pp. 87–91.
53. Most recently, see Ian Harris, 'The Politics of Christianity', in G.A.J. Rogers, *Locke's Philosophy: Content and Context* (Oxford, 1994), pp. 197–215, and Peter Schouls, *Reasoned Freedom* (Ithaca, NY, 1992).
54. W.M. Spellman, 'Archbishop John Tillotson and the Meaning of Moralism', *Anglican and Episcopal History*, 56 (1987), 404–22. See also Gerard Reedy, 'Interpreting Tillotson', *Harvard Theological Review*, 86 (1993), 81–104.
55. Marshall, *Locke*, pp. 131–6.
56. ST, 56. Cf. Joshua Mitchell, *Not by Reason Alone: Religion, History and Identity in Early Modern Political Thought* (Chicago, 1993), p. 86.
57. Locke to Lady E. Guise, Rotterdam, 21 June 1688, quoted in Yolton, *Locke and Way of Ideas*, p. 2.

4 Education into Humanity

1. ST, 63.
2. STCE, 103, 105. Nathan Tarkov, *Locke's Education for Liberty* (Chicago, 1984), p. 130, refers to the 'love of dominion' as one of the 'general propensities of human nature'.

3. STCE, no.70.
4. Correspondence, 3:999.
5. Correspondence, 4:1620. The composition of *Some Thoughts Concerning Education* is described in detail by James Axtell in his edition of *The Educational Writings of John Locke* (Cambridge, 1968), pp. 3–17.
6. John Yolton discusses each of these works in his introduction to the Clarendon edition of *Some Thoughts Concerning Education* (Oxford, 1989), pp. 8–12.
7. Neal Wood, *John Locke and Agrarian Capitalism* (Berkeley, CA, 1984), pp. 97–9. Statistical information on the English gentry from Marshall, *John Locke*, p. 158. For an overview of educational theory and practice in the seventeenth century, see Keith Wrightson, *English Society, 1580–1680* (London, 1982), pp. 183–221.
8. STCE, 'Epistle Dedicatory'.
9. Ibid, no.42.
10. The suggestion is made by Peter Schouls, *Reasoned Freedom*, pp. 180–1, fn.2. The paper is printed in H.R. Fox-Bourne, *The Life of John Locke*, 2 vols (London, 1876), 2:377–90. Compare A.L. Beier, 'Utter Strangers to Industry, Morality and Religion: John Locke on the Poor', *Eighteenth-Century Life*, 12 (1988), 28–41. Locke's comments on labour appear in Patrick Kelly (ed.), *Locke on Money* (Oxford, 1991), 2 vols, 2: 493–5. Tully's estimate of the working school proposal is contained in his essay 'Governing Conduct'. Neal Wood concurs with Tully's assessment (*Agrarian Capitalism*, 106–9) as I do in *Locke and the Problem of Depravity*, 206–10.
11. STCE, nos 136, 158, 159.
12. Wood, *Agrarian Capitalism*, pp. 102–6.
13. Patrick Kelly (ed.), *Locke on Money*, 2:493; Fox Bourne, *Life of Locke*, 2:378.
14. *Locke on Money*, 2:485, 1:176n, 1:40.
15. STCE, nos 1, 37.
16. Quoted in W.M. Spellman, 'The Christian Estimate of Man in Locke's *Essay*', *Journal of Religion*, 67, no. 4 (1987), 485.
17. Quoting John Dunn, *The Political Thought of John Locke* (Cambridge, 1968), p. 194.
18. STCE, no. 217.
19. Correspondence, 1:123.
20. 'Additions intended by the author to have been added to the Essay Concerning Human Understanding', printed in Lord King, *Life of Locke*, p. 360.
21. ST, 58. See also Uday Singh Mehta, *The Anxiety of Freedom: Imagination and Individuality in Locke's Political Thought* (Ithaca, NY, 1992), pp. 125–7; Edmund Leites, 'Locke's Liberal Theory of Parenthood', in Reinhard Brandt, *Locke: Symposium Wolfenbuttel* (New York, 1981), p. 94.
22. ECHU, 2.21.56.
23. Ibid., 4.19.14.
24. Ibid., 2.21.42.
25. Ibid., 2.21.43.
26. STCE, no. 33.
27. 'Concerning Education', in *The Miscellaneous Works of the Right Honourable Edward, Earl of Clarendon* (London, 1751), 315; STCE, no. 45.
28. Clarendon, *Miscellaneous Works*.
29. STCE, no. 41, p. 109.
30. See J.E. Stephens (ed.), *Aubrey on Education* (London, 1972), pp. 17–18. Locke allowed for corporal punishment in response to 'Stubborness, and an obstinate disobedience'.
31. ECHU, 2.28.7; 2.28.12.
32. STCE, no. 56.
33. STCE, no. 70.
34. Ibid.
35. ECHU, 4.20.8–10.

36. Ibid., 4.3.20.
37. For a discussion, see Alex Neill, 'Locke on Habituation, Autonomy, and Education', *Journal of the History of Philosophy*, 27 (1989), 225–45.
38. Ibid., 2.21.70.
39. STCE, no. 116.
40. Journal entry for 12 March 1677 quoted in Mark Glat, 'John Locke's Historical Sense' in Richard Ashcraft (ed.), *John Locke: Critical Assessments*, 4 vols (New York, 1991),3:624. I am indebted to Professor Glat's essay for much of what follows on Locke's view of history.
41. STCE, no. 116, 182, 184.
42. ST, no. 104
43. This according to W. von Leyden in his introduction to *Essays on the Law of Nature* (Oxford, 1954), p. 20.
44. STCE, no. 182.
45. See Peter Laslett (ed.), *Two Treatises of Government*, p. 65; J.G.A. Pocock, *The Ancient Constitution and the Feudal Law* (New York, 1967), p. 237.
46. Pocock, *Ancient Constitution*, p. 236, n. 2. Also 238. Idem, 'The Myth of John Locke and the Obsession with Liberalism', in *John Locke*, ed. Richard Ashcraft and John Pocock (Los Angeles, 1980), p. 4.
47. ST, no. 103.
48. ECHU, 3.9.22.
49. Paraphrase, preface, 1:103,104.
50. Lord King's 'Life of Locke' quoted in Glat, 'Locke's Historical Sense', p. 624; Correspondence, 6:2320.
51. 'Of Study', in Axtell (ed.), p. 422; ST, 107.
52. *Conduct of the Understanding*, ed. Thomas Fowler (New York, 1971), p. 22.
53. See Richard H. Popkin, *The History of Scepticism from Erasmus to Spinoza* (London, 1979), chs 1 and 10.
54. 'Of Study' in Axtell (ed.), p. 415.
55. ST, 55.
56. FT, 52,53; ST, 58,59. See Gordon Schochet, 'The Family and the Origins of the State in Locke's Political Philosophy', in John Yolton (ed.), *John Locke: Problems and Perspectives* (Cambridge, 1969), pp. 81–98.
57. ST, 60.
58. STCE, no. 38.

5 A Renewed Christian Politics

1. Jerome Huyler, *Locke in America* (Lawrence, KS, 1995); Steven M. Dworetz, *The Unvarnished Doctrine: Locke, Liberalism, and the American Revolution* (Durham, NC, 1990); and Thomas Pangle, *The Spirit of Modern Republicanism: The Moral Vision of the American Founders and the Philosophy of Locke* (Chicago, 1988) have each taken issue with recent historiography which discounts Locke's contribution to the American founding.
2. Dunn, *Political Thought of Locke*; Ashcraft, *Revolutionary Politics*; Geraint Parry, *John Locke* (London, 1978).
3. James Tully, *An Approach to Political Philosophy: Locke in Contexts* (Cambridge, 1993), p. 9. Also idem, 'Locke', in *The Cambridge History of Political Thought, 1450–1700*, ed. J.H. Burns (Cambridge, 1991), pp. 616–52.
4. For a brief but illuminating discussion see Rabb, *The Struggle for Stability in Early Modern Europe*.
5. Harris, *Mind of Locke*, pp. 11–12, 17–19.

6. ST, 4. In STCE, no. 117, Locke insisted that inferiors – in this case servants – are where they are because 'fortune has laid them below the level of others'.
7. For an overview of Filmer's thought, see Johann P. Sommerville (ed.), *Patriarcha and Other Writings* (Cambridge, 1991), Introduction.
8. Quoting Gordon J. Schochet, *Patriarchalism in Political Thought* (New York, 1975), p. 103. Wootton, *Political Writings of Locke*, p. 13, places the composition of *Patriarcha* around 1631 at the latest.
9. FT, 32.
10. FT, 145; *Two Tracts*, 171–2. For a discussion see N. Tarkov, *Locke's Education for Liberty* (Chicago, 1984), p. 62.
11. FT, 3, 6. See also Tully's discussion in *Discourse on Property*, pp. 157–8.
12. FT, 67. Cf. *A Letter Concerning Toleration*, ed. James Tully (Indianapolis, 1983), p. 36.
13. ST, 6, 23, 135.
14. *Two Tracts*, pp. 160–1.
15. Spellman, *Locke and the Problem of Depravity*, pp. 50–5.
16. Marvell quoted in Mark Goldie, 'John Locke and Anglican Royalism', *Political Studies*, 31 (1983), 63.
17. Preface to *Two Treatises*, p. 172.
18. *Letter Concerning Toleration*, p. 23. The *Letter* was a translation of the *Epistola de tolerantia*. The translator was William Popple.
19. John Dunn, 'What is Living and What is Dead in the Political Theory of John Locke?', in Dunn, *Interpreting Political Responsibility* (Princeton, NJ, 1990), p. 19.
20. *Letter Concerning Toleration*, pp. 23, 27, 28, 30, 36.
21. Ashcraft, *Revolutionary Politics*. The argument was first presented in 'Revolutionary Politics and Locke's Two Treatises of Government', *Political Theory*, 8 (1980), 429–86.
22. David Wootton offers a third dating for the Second Treatise, mid to late 1681. See his discussion in *Locke's Political Writings*, pp. 49–89.
23. ST, 19; Marshall, ch. 6, pp. 205–91. Gordon Schochet, 'Radical Politics and Ashcraft's Treatise on Locke', *Journal of the History of Ideas*, 50 (1989), 491–510, also takes exception to the claim that Locke was appealing to lower class radicals.
24. Tyrrell, *Biblioteca Politica*, quoted in Tully, 'Locke', in *Cambridge History*, p. 639.
25. J.P. Kenyon, *Revolution Principles: The Politics of Party, 1689–1720* (Cambridge, 1977), pp. 7–20.
26. William G. Batz, 'The Historical Anthropology of John Locke', *Journal of the History of Ideas*, 35 (1974), 663–70.
27. ST, 4–6.
28. Hobbes, *Leviathan* (Cambridge, 1991), ch.13.
29. ST, 5, 6, 12, 15, 136.
30. ST, 123.
31. ST, 199.
32. ST, 3.
33. Proponents of this view include C.B. Macpherson, *The Political Philosophy of Possessive Individualism* (Oxford, 1962) and Leo Strauss, *Natural Right and History* (Chicago, 1953).
34. Quoted in Harris, *Mind of Locke*, p. 225.
35. ST, 5.
36. Wood, *Locke and Agrarian Capitalism*, p. 101.
37. Tully, *A Discourse on Property*, pp. 150–1.
38. FT, 86, 87–92. In ST, 16, Locke says that the preservation of man is the 'Fundamental Law of Nature'.
39. Fox-Bourne, *Life of Locke*, 2:382–3.
40. Richard Tuck, *Natural Rights Theories: Their Origins and Development* (Cambridge, 1979), p. 172; Ashcraft, 'Locke's Political Philosophy' in Vere Chappell (ed.), *The*

Cambridge Companion to Locke, pp. 242–3; W. von Leyden, *Hobbes and Locke: The Politics of Freedom and Obligation* (New York, 1982), p. 105. Ramon M. Lemos, 'Locke's Theory of Property', *Interpretations*, 5 (1975), 226–44; Kristin Shrader-Frechette, 'Locke and Limits on Land Ownership', *Journal of the History of Ideas*, 54 (1993), 201–19.

41. STCE, no. 110. This passage is quoted in the conclusion of James Tully's *A Discourse on Property* (Cambridge, 1980), p. 176.

42. ST, 6.

43. I owe what follows on Locke and Amerindians to James Tully's insightful 'Rediscovering America: the Two Treatises and aboriginal rights', in *An Approach to Political Philosophy*, pp. 137–76, and to Herman Lebovics, 'The Uses of America in Locke's Second Treatise', *Journal of the History of Ideas*, 47 (1986), 567–81.

44. Francis Jennings, *The Invasion of America: Indians, Colonialism and the Cant of Conquest* (New York, 1975), pp. 105–28.

45. ST, 34.

46. Works, 10:196.

47. Works, 10:196.

48. Wayne Glausser, 'Three Approaches to Locke and the Slave Trade', *Journal of the History of Ideas*, 51, no. 2 (1990), 199–216, discusses the problem of interpretation in detail.

49. Dunn, *Political Thought of Locke*, p. 175, n. 4. Geraint Parry, *John Locke*, p. 70; James Farr, ' "So Vile and Miserable an Estate": The Problem of Slavery in Locke's Political Thought', *Political Theory*, 14 (1986), 263–89.

50. David Hume, 'On the Original Contract', in *The Philosophical Works of David Hume*, 4 vols (London, 1826), 3:531–2.

6   An Enlightenment Legacy

1. Pierre Coste, 'The Character of Mr. Locke', in *A Collection of Several Pieces of Mr. John Locke* (London, 1720), pp. xxi–xxii; Correspondence, 8:3648; Cranston, *John Locke*, pp. 481–2, reproduces Locke's epitaph.

2. Quoting Donald Greene, 'Augustinianism and Empiricism: A Note on Eighteenth-Century English Intellectual History', *Eighteenth-Century Studies*, 1 (1967–8): 52.

3. *Conduct* in *Works*, 3 vols (London, 1727), 3:407, no. 22.

4. ECHU, 1.1.6; 1.1.7.

5. Paul Hazard, *The European Mind, 1680–1715*, trans. J. Lewis May (New York, 1964), p. 288.

6. See G.A.J. Rogers' introduction to the modern edition of Wynne's *An Abridgement of Mr. Locke's Essay Concerning Human Understanding* (Bristol, 1990).

7. Rosalie L. Colie, 'John Locke and the Publication of the Private', *Philological Quarterly*, 45 (1966), 24.

8. For the complete publishing history of Locke's works, see John C. Attig, *The Works of John Locke: A Comprehensive Bibliography from the Seventeenth Century to the Present* (Westport, CT, 1985).

9. Watts, *Philosophical Essays* (London, 1733), Essay no. 6.

10. Cragg, *Reason and Authority in the Eighteenth Century* (Cambridge, 1964), p. 3.

11. Neal Wood, 'Tabula Rasa, Social Environmentalism, and the "English Paradigm" ', *Journal of the History of Ideas*, 53 (1992), 647–68.

12. Helvetius quoted in Peter Gay, *The Enlightenment*, 2 vols (New York, 1967), 2:512.

13. Quoting Samuel F. Pickering, Jr, *John Locke and Children's Books in Eighteenth-Century England* (Knoxville, TN, 1981), p. 12. Peter Gay (ed.), *John Locke on Education* (New

York, 1964), p. 1, stated that Locke 'was the father of the Enlightenment in educational thought as in so much else'.

14. Chamber's *Cyclopaedia*, 4 vols, 2nd edn (London, 1738), entry on education, vol. 1; Pickering, *Locke and Children's Books*, p. 16; David Spadafora, *The Idea of Progress in Eighteenth-Century Britain* (New Haven, CT, 1990), pp. 167–78.

15. STCE, no. 61; 'Of Study' in Axtell (ed.), *Educational Writings of Locke*, p. 411.

16. Clarke, *Essay Upon Education of Youth in Grammar Schools*, 2nd edn (London, 1730), pp. 3–7. Clarke, *An Essay Upon Study* (London, 1731), pp. 148–50.

17. Hendley and Nelson quoted in Victor E. Neuburg, *Popular Education in Eighteenth Century England* (London, 1971), p. 7.

18. Watts, *An Essay Towards the Encouragement of Charity Schools* 1728, in Neuburg, pp. 8–9.

19. Watts, *Improvement of the Mind* (Edinburgh, 1801), p. 4.

20. *Fable of the Bees* (Oxford, 1924), 2.190.

21. Lawrence Cremin, *American Education: The Colonial Experience, 1607–1783* (New York, 1970), p. 277; STCE, no. 135.

22. Burgh quoted in ibid., p. 285.

23. STCE, no. 136.

24. Shepard, *Essay on Education* (London, 1782), p. 17, quoted in Spadafora, *Idea of Progress*, p. 172.

25. Carroll, *A Dissertation upon the Tenth Chapter of the Fourth Book of Mr. Locke's Essay, Concerning Human Understanding* (London, 1706), p. 276.

26. See John Yolton, *Way of Ideas*, p. 181. Kenneth MacLean, *John Locke and English Literature of the Eighteenth-Century* (New York, 1962), pp. 5–6, also stresses that Locke's work was heavily criticized 'in pulpit and pamphlet'.

27. Burnet, *History of My Own Time*, 6 vols (Oxford, 1833), 4:387.

28. See John Yolton, *Thinking Matter*, and Yolton, 'French Materialist Disciples of Locke', *Journal of the History of Ideas* (1987), 83–104. According to Nicholas Jolley, *Leibniz and Locke: A Study of the New Essays on Human Understanding* (Oxford, 1984), p. 7, 'The chief focus of Leibniz's hostility to Locke's philosophy is what he takes to be its pervasively materialist tendency'.

29. ECHU, 4.3.6.

30. *Letters Concerning the English Nation* (London, 1733), pp. 100–3.

31. Joseph Priestly, in *Disquisitions Relating to Matter and Spirit* (London, 1777), p. 218.

32. Will Lupton, *The Resurrection of the Same Body* (Oxford, 1711); Winch Holdsworth, *A Sermon Preached before the University of Oxford at St. Mary's on Easter Monday* (London, 1720); Henry Felton, *The Resurrection of the Same Numerical Body* (Oxford, 1725).

33. Catherine Cockburn, *A Letter to Dr. Holdsworth, Occasioned by His Sermon Preached before the University of Oxford* (London, 1726); Holdsworth, *A Defense of the Doctrine of the Resurrection of the Same Body* (London, 1727).

34. Isaac Watts, *Philosophical Essays*, 3rd edn (London, 1742), pp. 183, 188, 190.

35. Sherlock quoted in Cragg, *Reason and Authority*, p. 51.

36. On William's role see Spellman, *Latitudinarians*, pp. 135–6; G.V. Bennett, 'King William III and the Episcopate', in Bennett and J.D. Walsh (eds), *Essays in Modern Church History* (Oxford, 1966), p. 115.

37. Correspondence, 3:1131.

38. Correspondence, 3:1147.

39. Hugh Trevor-Roper, 'Toleration and Religion after 1688', in *From Persecution to Toleration*, p. 390. I am indebted to Professor Trevor-Roper's essay, and to Nicholas Tyacke, 'The Rise of Puritanism and the Legalizing of Dissent, 1571–1719' in the same volume, for much of what follows.

40. Correspondence, 3:1147.

41. Martyn P. Thompson, 'The Reception of Locke's *Two Treatises of Government*, 1690–1705', *Political Studies*, 24 (1976), 184–91; Kenyon, *Revolution Politics*, pp. 5–21.

42. Patrick Kelly, 'William Molyneux and the Spirit of Liberty in Eighteenth-Century Ireland', *Eighteenth-Century Ireland*, vol. 3 (1988), pp. 133–48. Molyneux indiscreetly mentioned Locke as the author of *Two Treatises*. See *The Case of Ireland's being Bound by Acts of Parliament in England, Stated* (Dublin, 1698), p. 153.

43. John Miller, *Origins of the American Revolution* (Boston, 1943), p.170. Merle Curti, 'The Great Mr. Locke, America's Philosopher', *Huntington Library Bulletin*, 11 (1939). See also Carl Becker, *The Declaration of Independence* (New York, 1942).

44. Bernard Bailyn, *The Ideological Origins of the American Revolution* (Cambridge, MA, 1967); Gordon Wood, *The Creation of the American Republic* (New York, 1973).

45. David Wootton (ed.), *Republicanism, Liberty, and Commercial Society, 1649–1776* (Stanford, CA, 1994), Introduction, pp. 8–10.

46. John Pocock, *The Machiavellian Moment: Florentine Political Thought and the Atlantic Republican Tradition* (Princeton, NJ, 1975); idem, 'Virtue and Commerce', in *Politics, Language, and Time: Essays on Political Thought and History* (New York, 1971), p. 144.

47. Quoted in Dunn, 'The Politics of Locke in England and America', in John Yolton (ed.), *John Locke: Problems and Perspectives* (Cambridge, 1969), p. 78, n. 1. A recent endorsement of the revisionist thesis can be found in Oscar and Lilian Handlin, 'Who Read John Locke? Words and Acts in the American Revolution' *The American Scholar*, 58 (1989), 545–56.

48. Dworetz, *The Unvarnished Doctrine: Locke, Liberalism, and the American Revolution*.

49. In addition to Dworetz, see Huyler, *Locke in America*; Pangle, *Spirit of Modern Republicanism*; Donald Lutz, *The Origins of American Constitutionalism* (Baton Rouge, LA, 1988); Isaac Kramnick, 'Republican Revisionism Revisited', *American Historical Review*, 87 (1982), 629–64.

50. Turner quoted in Dworetz, p. 178; Thomas Jefferson to Benjamin Rush, in Saul K. Padover (ed.), *Thomas Jefferson on Democracy* (New York, 1939), p. 108.

51. Locke, *A Letter Concerning Toleration* in Tully (ed.), p. 47.

Conclusion

1. *A Letter Concerning Toleration*, p. 47; Works, 6.41, 42.

BIBLIOGRAPHY

The best and most direct source for the study of Locke is the Clarendon Edition of *The Works of John Locke*, formerly edited by Peter Nidditch and John Yolton, and currently under the general supervision of G.A.J. Rogers. The Clarendon Edition is an on-going project and represents the first effort to publish the key texts in the Locke corpus in over 150 years. Already published are Peter Nidditch's edition of the *Essay Concerning Human Understanding* (1975); John and Jean Yolton's edition of *Some Thoughts Concerning Education* (1989); Esmund S. De Beer's eight-volume edition of *The Correspondence of John Locke* (1979–89); Arthur Wainwright's edition of *A Paraphrase and Notes on the Epistles of St. Paul*, 2 vols (1987); Patrick Kelly's edition of Locke's writings on financial matters, *Locke on Money*, 2 vols (1991); and *Drafts for the Essay Concerning Human Understanding and Other Philosophical Writings*, ed. Peter Nidditch and G.A.J. Rogers.

Other key modern editions of works, papers, and journal entries by Locke, not currently available as part of the Clarendon project, include Phillip Abram's edition of the *Two Tracts on Government* (Cambridge, 1967); Peter Laslett's critical edition of *Two Treatises of Government* (Cambridge, 1963; 1987); Wolfgang von Leyden's edition of *Essays On the Law of Nature* (Oxford, 1954); *Questions on the Law of Nature* (Ithaca, NY, 1990), ed. R. Horowitz, J.S. Clay, and D. Clay; *Locke's Travels in France* (Cambridge, 1953), ed. John Lough; *Locke's Conduct of the Understanding* (New York, 1882; 1971), ed. Thomas Fowler; and James Tully's edition of *A Letter Concerning Toleration* (Indianapolis, 1983).

John Attig's *The Works of John Locke* (Westport, CT, 1985) provides a listing of editions of Locke's published works. Roland Hall and Roger Woolhouse's *Eighty Years of Locke Scholarship* (Edinburgh, 1985) covers the secondary literature on Locke; it should be supplemented with the annual updates contained in the *Locke Newsletter*. The Yoltons' *John Locke: A Reference Guide* (Boston, 1985) contains works on Locke from the late seventeenth century until 1982. Two essential books, John Marshall, *Locke: Resistance, Religion and Responsibility* (Cambridge, 1994) and Ian Harris, *The Mind of John Locke* (Cambridge, 1994) both include extensive bibliographies of primary literature by Locke's contemporary critics and supporters. P. Long, *A Summary Catalogue of the Lovelace Collection of the Papers of John Locke in the Bodleian Library* (Oxford, 1959) describes the manuscript collection, while Peter Laslett and John Gough have edited *The Library Catalogue of John Locke* (Oxford, 1965).

The following list of secondary literature samples mainly the scholarship produced over the last 40 years, since the opening of the Lovelace collection of Locke manuscripts. In order to assist those who would like to examine particular issues in more detail, it includes some entries which do not appear in the notes.

Almond, P., *Heaven and Hell in the English Enlightenment* (Cambridge, 1994).

Appleby, J., *Liberalism and Republicanism in the Historical Imagination* (Cambridge, 1992).

Ashcraft, R., *Revolutionary Politics and Locke's 'Two Treatises of Government'* (Princeton, NJ, 1986).

Ashcraft, R., *Locke's 'Two Treatises of Government'* (London, 1987).

Ashcraft, R. (ed.), *John Locke: Critical Assessments*, 4 vols (London, 1991).

Bibliography 157

Ashcraft, R., Kroll, R., and Zagorin, P. (eds), *Philosophy, Science and Religion in England 1640–1700* (Cambridge, 1992).
Ayers, M., *Locke: Epistemology and Ontology* 2 vols (New York, 1993).
Beier, A.L., 'Utter Strangers to Industry, Morality and Religion: John Locke on the Poor', *Eighteenth Century Life*, 12 (1988), 28–41.
Biddle, J., 'Locke's Critique of Innate Principles and Toland's Deism', *Journal of the History of Ideas*, 37 (1976), 410–22.
Bill, E.G.W. *Education at Christ Church, Oxford, 1650–1800* (Oxford, 1988).
Bonney, R., *The European Dynastic States* (Oxford, 1991).
Brandt, R. (ed.), *John Locke: Symposium Wolfenbuettel* (Berlin, 1979).
Braur, G.L., *The Education of a Gentleman: Theories of Gentlemanly Education in England, 1660–1675* (New York, 1959).
Burns, J.H. (ed.), *The Cambridge History of Political Thought, 1450–1700* (Cambridge, 1991).
Burns, N.T., *Christian Mortalism from Tyndale to Milton* (Cambridge, MA, 1972).
Carroll, R.T., *The Commonsense Philosophy of Bishop Edward Stillingfleet* (The Hague, 1975).
Chambliss, J.J., 'Reason, Conduct and Revelation in the Educational Theory of Locke, Watts and Burgh', *Educational Theory*, 26 (1976), 372–87.
Champion, J., *The Pillars of Priestcraft Shaken* (Cambridge, 1992).
Chappell, V. (ed.), *The Cambridge Companion to Locke* (Cambridge, 1994).
Chappell, V., 'Locke on the Intellectual Basis of Sin', *Journal of the History of Philosophy*, 32 (1994), 197–207.
Clark, J.C.D., *English Society, 1688–1832* (Cambridge, 1985).
Colman, J., *John Locke's Moral Philosophy* (Edinburgh, 1983).
Cox, R., *Locke on War and Peace* (Oxford, 1960).
Cragg, G.R., *Reason and Authority in the Eighteenth Century* (Cambridge, 1964).
Cranston, M., *John Locke: A Biography* (London, 1957).
Cremin, L., *American Education: The Colonial Experience* (New York, 1978).
Curti, M., 'The Great Mr. Locke: America's Philosopher', *Huntington Library Bulletin*, 11 (1937), 107–51.
Davies, H., *Worship and Theology in England, 1603–1690* (Princeton, NJ, 1975).
Dewhurst, K., *John Locke: Physician and Philosopher* (London, 1963).
Dunn, J., *The Political Thought of John Locke* (Cambridge, 1969).
Dunn, J., *Locke* (Oxford, 1984).
Dworetz, S., *The Unvarnished Doctrine: Locke, Liberalism and the American Revolution* (Durham, 1990).
Fox-Bourne, H.R., *The Life of John Locke*, 2 vols (New York, 1876).
Franklin, J., *John Locke and the Theory of Sovereignty* (Cambridge, 1978).
Goldie, M., 'John Locke's Circle and James II', *Historical Journal*, 35 (1992), 557–86.
Goldie, M., 'John Locke and Anglican Royalism', *Political Studies*, 31 (1983), 61–5.
Gough, J.W., *John Locke's Political Philosophy* (Oxford, 1956).
Gough, J.W., 'James Tyrrell, Whig Historian and Friend of John Locke', *Historical Journal*, 19 (1976), 541–60.
Grant, R., *John Locke's Liberalism* (Chicago, 1987).
Grell, O.P. (ed.), *From Persecution to Toleration: The Glorious Revolution and Religion in England* (Oxford, 1991).
Haley, K.H.D., *The First Earl of Shaftesbury* (Oxford, 1968).
Handlin, O. and Handlin, L., 'Who Read John Locke? Words and Acts in the American Revolution', *The American Scholar*, 58 (1989), 545–56.
Harpham, E.J. (ed.), *John Locke's 'Two Treatises': New Interpretations* (Lawrence, Kansas, 1992).
Harris, I., *The Mind of John Locke* (Cambridge, 1994).
Harris, T., *London Crowds in the Reign of Charles II* (Cambridge, 1987).
Harris, T. (ed.), *The Politics of Religion in Restoration England* (Oxford, 1990).

Horwitz, H., 'Protestant Reconciliation during the Exclusion Crisis', *Journal of Ecclesiastical History*, 15 (1964), 201–17.

Hundert, E.J., 'The Making of Homo Faber: John Locke between Ideology and History', *Journal of the History of Ideas*, 33 (1972), 3–22.

Hunter, M., *Science and Society in Restoration England* (Cambridge, 1981).

Hunter, M. and Wootton, D. (eds), *Atheism from the Reformation to the Enlightenment* (Oxford, 1992).

Hutton, R., *The Restoration* (Oxford, 1983).

Johnson, M.S., *Locke on Freedom* (Austin, TX, 1977).

Jolley, N., *Locke and Leibniz* (Oxford, 1984).

Kemering, G., 'Locke on the Essence of the Soul', *Southern Journal of Philosophy*, 17 (1979), 455–64.

Kramnick, I., *Republicanism and Bourgeois Radicalism: Political Ideology in Late Eighteenth-Centurry England and America* (Ithaca, NY, 1990).

Lutz, D., *The Origins of American Constitutionalism* (Baton Rouge, LA, 1988).

Mabbott, J.D., *John Locke* (Oxford, 1980).

McAdoo, H.R., *The Spirit of Anglicanism* (London, 1965).

McGee. J., *The Godly Man in Stuart England* (New Haven, CT, 1976).

McLachlan, H., *Socinianism in Seventeenth-Century England* (Oxford, 1951).

Maclean, K., *John Locke and English Literature of the Eighteenth Century* (New Haven, CT, 1936).

Macpherson, C.B., *The Theory of Possessive Individualism: Hobbes to Locke* (Oxford, 1962).

Marshall, J., *Locke: Resistance, Revolution and Responsibility* (Cambridge, 1994).

Mehta, U.S., *The Anxiety of Freedom: Imagination and Individuality in Locke's Political Thought* (Ithaca, NY, 1992).

Mendus, S., *Toleration and the Limits of Liberalism* (London, 1989).

Miller, J., *Popery and Politics in England, 1660–1688* (Cambridge, 1973).

Miller, J., *James II* (Hove, Sussex, 1978).

Mitchell, J., *Not by Reason Alone: Religion, History and Identity in Early Modern Political Thought* (Chicago, 1993).

Montuouri, M., *John Locke on Toleration and the Unity of God* (Amsterdam, 1983).

Neill, A., 'Locke on Habituation, Autonomy, and Education', *Journal of the History of Philosophy*, 27 (1989), 225–45.

Ogg, D., *England in the Reign of Charles II* (Oxford, 1934).

Ogg, D., *England in the Reigns of James II and William III* (Oxford, 1969).

Pangle, T., *The Spirit of Modern Republicanism* (Chicago, 1988).

Parry, G., *Locke* (London, 1973).

Passmore, J., 'Locke and the Ethics of Belief', *Proceedings of the British Academy*, 64 (1978), 185–208.

Pickering, S.F., *John Locke and Children's Books in Eighteenth-Century England* (Knoxville, TN, 1981).

Pocock, J.G.A., *The Ancient Constitution and the Feudal Law* (Cambridge, 1957; 1987).

Popkin, R.H., 'The Philosophy of Edward Stillingfleet', *Journal of the History of Philosophy*, 9 (1971), 303–19.

Popkin, R.H., *The History of Scepticism: Erasmus to Spinoza* (London, 1979).

Quintana, R., *Two Augustans: John Locke and Jonathan Swift* (Madison, WI, 1978).

Rabb, T., *The Struggle for Stability in Early Modern Europe* (New York, 1975).

Rabich, M.S., 'The Reasonableness of Locke, or the Questionableness of Christianity', *Journal of Politics*, 53 (1991), 933–57.

Redwood, J., *Reason, Ridicule and Religion* (London, 1976).

Reedy, G., 'Interpreting Tillotson', *Harvard Theological Review*, 63 (1993), 81–103.

Reedy, G., *The Bible and Reason* (Philadelphia, 1985).

Rogers, G.A.J., 'Boyle, Locke and Reason', *Journal of the History of Ideas*, 27 (1966), 205–16.

Rogers, G.A.J. (ed.), *Locke's Philosophy: Content and Context* (Oxford, 1994).

Romanell, P., *John Locke and Medicine: A New Key to Locke* (Buffalo, NY, 1984).
Rupp, G., *Religion in England, 1688–1791* (Oxford, 1986).
Schlatter, R., *The Social Ideas of Religious Leaders, 1660–1688* (Oxford, 1940).
Schochet, G., *Patriarchalism in Political Thought* (Oxford, 1975).
Schochet, G., 'Toleration, Revolution and Judgment in the Development of Locke's Political Thought', *Political Science*, 40 (1988), 84–96.
Schochet, G., 'Aschcraft on Locke', *Journal of the History of Ideas*, 3 (1989), 491–510.
Schouls, P., *Reasoned Freedom: John Locke and Enlightenment* (Ithaca, NY, 1992).
Scott, J., *Algernon Sydney and the Restoration Crisis, 1677–1683* (Cambridge, 1991).
Seaward, P., *The Restoration* (London, 1990).
Seliger, M., *The Liberal Politics of John Locke* (London, 1968).
Shapiro, B., *Probability and Certainty in Seventeenth-Century England* (Princeton, NJ, 1983).
Simmons, A.J., *The Lockean Theory of Rights* (Princeton, NJ, 1992).
Simmons, A.J., *On the Edge of Anarchy: Locke, Consent and the Limits of Society* (Princeton, NJ, 1993).
Snook, I.A., 'John Locke's Moral Theory of Education', *Educational Theory*, 20 (1976), 364–7.
Snyder, D., 'Faith and Reason in Locke's *Essay*', *Journal of the History of Ideas*, 47 (1986), 197–213.
Sommerville, J.P., *The Secularization of Early Modern England* (Oxford, 1992).
Spellman, W.M., *John Locke and the Problem of Depravity* (Oxford, 1988).
Spellman, W.M., *The Latitudinarians and the Church of England, 1660–1700* (Athens, GA, 1993).
Spellman, W.M., 'Between Death and Judgment: Conflicting Images of the Afterlife in Seventeenth-Century English Eulogies', *Harvard Theological Review*, 87 (1994), 49–66.
Spellman, W.M., 'Bishop Jeremy Taylor and the Anglican Dilemma of the Dead Awaiting Resurrection', *Anglican and Episcopal History*, 63 (1994), 49–65.
Spellman, W.M., 'Archbishop John Tillotson and the Meaning of Moralism', *Anglican and Episcopal History*, 56 (1987), 404–22.
Spurr, J., *The Restoration Church of England* (New Haven, CT, 1991).
Stewart, M.A., 'Locke's Professional Contacts with Robert Boyle', *Locke Newsletter*, 12 (1981), 19–44.
Strauss, L., *Natural Right and History* (Chicago, 1953).
Sullivan, R., *John Toland and the Deist Controversy* (Cambridge, MA, 1982).
Tarkov, N., *Locke's Education for Liberty* (Chicago, 1984).
Thomas, K., *Religion and the Decline of Magic* (Harmondsworth, 1984).
Thompson, M.P., 'The Reception of Locke's *Two Treatises of Government*, 1690–1705', *Political Studies*, 24 (1976), 184–91.
Tuck, R., *Natural Rights Theories: Their Origin and Development* (Cambridge, 1979).
Tully, J., *A Discourse on Property* (Cambridge, 1980).
Tully, J., *An Approach to Political Philosophy: Locke in Contexts* (Cambridge, 1993).
Van Leeuwen, H.G., *The Problem of Certainty in English Thought, 1630–1690* (The Hague, 1970).
Von Leyden, W., *Hobbes and Locke: The Politics of Freedom and Obligation* (New York, 1982).
Walker, D.P., *The Decline of Hell* (Chicago, 1964).
Wallace, D.D., 'Socinianism, Justification by Faith, and the Sources of John Locke's *The Reasonableness of Christianity*', *Journal of the History of Ideas*, 45 (1984), 49–66.
Walmsley, P., 'Dispute and Conversation: Probability and the Rhetoric of Natural Philosophy in Locke's *Essay*', *Journal of the History of Ideas*, 54 (1993), 381–94.
Walsh, J. (ed.), *The Church of England 1689–1833: From Toleration to Tracterianism* (Oxford, 1992).
Westfall, R., *Science and Religion in Seventeenth-Century England* (Ann Arbor, MI, 1973).
Willey, B., *The Seventeenth-Century Background* (London, 1934).
Wood, N., *The Politics of Locke's Philosophy* (Berkeley, CA, 1983).

Wood, N., *John Locke and Agrarian Capitalism* (Berkeley, CA, 1984).

Wood, N., 'Tabula Rasa, Social Environmentalism, and the "English Paradigm"', *Journal of the History of Ideas*, 53 (1992), 647–68.

Woolhouse, R.S., *John Locke* (Brighton, 1983).

Wootton, D., 'John Locke: Socinian or Natural Law Theorist?', in J. Crimmins (ed.), *Religion, Secularization and Political Thought: Thomas Hobbes to J.S. Mill* (London, 1989), pp. 39–67.

Wootton, D. (ed.), *Political Writings of John Locke* (New York, 1993).

Wrightson, K., *English Society, 1580–1680* (London, 1982).

Yolton, Jean (ed.), *A Locke Miscellany* (Bristol, 1990).

Yolton, John, *John Locke and the Way of Ideas* (Oxford, 1956).

Yolton, John (ed.), *John Locke: Problems and Perspectives* (Cambridge, 1969).

Yolton, John, *John Locke and the Compass of Human Understanding* (Cambridge, 1970).

Yolton, John, *John Locke: An Introduction* (Oxford, 1985).

Yolton, John, *A Locke Dictionary* (Oxford, 1990).

INDEX